T0365664

Random Thoughts

Donald Hoelscher

ISBN: 978-1-4269-5221-0 (sc)
ISBN: 978-1-4269-5222-7 (e)

Trafford rev. 12/09/2010

 www.trafford.com

North America & international
toll-free: 1 888 232 4444 (USA & Canada)
phone: 250 383 6864 ♦ fax: 812 355 4082

A Dream

Wouldn't it be nice to see all the world at peace and see people on earth greet each other with a sign of peace and see the starving people with plenty to eat and home's for the homeless with some place to sleep and warm clothes for all on the street and health care for the sick children and all those in need and churches full of people for the Lord there to greet for Easter the time to rejoice in the Lord and remember the reason for Easter this year

By Donald Hoelscher

A Fallen Star

*I met a girl one time that I knew I just had
to have she was the only one that I knew I
wanted for all my life its funny that once I
heard a song that talked About a star that fell
from the heavens above this girl was my star
my only world my one true love and I knew
my life was complete but like the song did say
one day she died and went away and I lost
part of my heart and still feel that today*

By Donald Hoelscher

A Teachers Wit

*The teachers wit is their best tool for it takes
some wit for them to rule and to teach the
kids is the right idea but kids are funny
and some time don't listen and if you want
their attention ask an off the wall question
something they don't expect that makes them
think oh what the heck so if to teach is your
desire a little more wit goes a long long way*

By Donald Hoelscher

Alarm Clock

*It's time to get up and face another day but
my body says no there is no way that sleep
was fleeting and I have to work all day and
it will be and effort there's got to be another
way to stay in bed so just go away and forget
the time tomorrow's another day by then I'll
be ready or so they say but I am not sure and
I need my pay so I had best get up and get on
my way*

By Donald Hoelscher

All That Glitters

Sometime as we hear the news we hear the promises by some fools of what they say that they will do but if the truth be on their tongue than maybe starvation and poverty would be on the run but we all know that talk is cheap for we see things that make us weep like family's living on the street and kids with nothing left to eat I think it's time we do our part and give the people another start

By Donald Hoelscher

Alligator

There was a time in a boy's life when he thought if he didn't soon find him a wife he'd buy an alligator instead of a wife but little does he know that they are almost the same and both will chew on your blank and hold you to blame so the morel of this poem is take the lesser of the two and find you a wife to take care of you

By Donald Hoelscher

Alone

*To be alone is not so hot for it makes you
realize what you're not and think about your
life back in the past and wonder why it didn't
last, and little things just seem to pitch you
back into a big old ditch. were you wallow in
your thoughts about what you had and now
do not, a person you can call your friend to
stay with you until the end and to be with you
most every day and share each other's pain
and gripes and cuddle with you every night
so ill end this poem in this way to be alone is
not the way*

By Donald Hoelscher

Alone Again

*As I sit in this house alone I think of the past
and wonder about the future and what kind
of a life I still have in store and what life is
going to bring me I see my old friends going
downhill every day and I wonder if this is
what I have in store for me and contemplate
my future and what I will be doing in the
future if I have one any way so that's enough
of this put me down its time to get up and go
to town*

By Donald Hoelscher

Alone and Confused

I get up each morning alone and confused and try very hard to lose these old blues it seems to me that there has got to be more to life than to be all alone with no companion or wife some time I wonder what this worlds coming to and I think of the past and where it's gone to I know each of us has their own story to tell but to be alone is our own living hell so the morel of this story is this find you a mate and don't try to resist and make a mistake

By Donald Hoelscher

American

I vote every year I pay my taxes never fear I stand up for what is right I serve my country in its fight but there are some things I don't quite understand why people on the street do stand we seem to have money for this and that but to help our people that's too bad we elect our people to serve our needs but listen to the news and greave for the money goes to parks and things and buildings too I am sure they will do very well for they don't eat and they don't starve so tell those people in the place up there to start with people on the street that's more than fair

By Donald Hoelscher

Animals

There is a thought I had last night about some animals that got in to a fight and as the fight soon progressed the smallest one was getting the best of the fight if you take this story and compare it to our lives we can see that the it's not so far from the truth the world that we now live in today is like the story that's all I can say the one that is starting to get the best of the fight is me and you and its well overdue the biggest animal is the bankers and big business now that our Uncle Sam has entered the fight there all squealing and moaning the blues for now its them that's starting to loose

By Donald Hoelscher

Another Blue Monday

*There are songs written about this day and
the things they say are true today for there
is no way to hold this head that doesn't hurt
and chances you are you'll run into some kind
of jerk that so big on him or herself that that
there ain't no way to get along that's all I'll
say it's said that animals fight and squabble
but the bottom line is they don't make trouble
for the ones who are creatures like them and
they stand beside them like they began*

By Donald Hoelscher

Another day

As I sit here in the solitude of this house that once was the place of joy for my first wife and family I am reminded of the past and all the good times shared with family and friends and how the life I had turned into and ever sliding place of sorrow and depression of loss of kids through death and marriage and as each day passes I look for a place, and a friend wife and lover or companion as the wife's I had left in death or divorce and now I am alone there is no recourse but to be alone or find someone else and when you're are still in love with the one who left that makes it harder to not be alone so all I can say is be careful of your heart be sure before you give it away

By Donald Hoelscher

Anxiety

Did you ever have a time when things seen
to happen and you wonder what's next but
there is no one there to answer so you stumble
around in your mind looking for the answer
but there is no way to solve the dilemma that
you have found yourself in so you continue
to talk to yourself but if you have you'll
understand that the one you talk to is the
same as the one who has the problem

By Donald Hoelscher

As I Sat

*I was in town just the other day and decided
to go for something to eat and as I sat there
quite alone I listed to the talk that drifted
around its hard to sit in a crowd and not to
hear the things that you can readily hear one
was fishing the other one kids another was
work that disappeared   politics was an issue
there too about the things that's happing to
me and you and so to end this I would agree
that the BS was prevalent for all to hear and
see*

By Donald Hoelscher

As I Sit

*As I sit here all alone I think about this house
and home of things that happened long ago
and people that I do know and places that I
used to go and fun I had way back then and
wonder where to begin again*

By Donald Hoelscher

Bad Day

*This day begin as normal as could be than
as the day wore on I have to say it went from
good to a lousy day for things began to go
from bad to worse and let me tell you with
song and verse went to wall mart to buy some
oil and a filter for my little car took off the
filter drained the oil put in the plug and the
new filter to but when the car started I am
telling you oil was coming out right and left
we checked the filter and to our regret the
gasket that was supposed to be there was
nowhere in sight so to wall mart we took our
plight we got a new filter and oil to now I am
happy how about you*

By Donald Hoelscher

Bad Morning

*I got up this morning and don't you know I
found a tick where a tick shouldn't go and the
mirror I thought I had has gone somewhere
and that made it bad and the tweezers I had
just wouldn't work so I pondered on going
on to work so I finally did and wouldn't you
know a dog ran out in front of the car and so
I swerved to miss the dog and when I finally
got to work I pulled up and stopped with a
jerk and thought if this is the way my day
began I shudder to think how my day will
end*

By Donald Hoelscher

Bad Night

*Last night as I tossed and turned in my sleep
I had a dream that made me keep on the edge
of my sleep thinking about the world so mean
and of things that were to change and why it
was so deranged I saw schools closing down
and people stair and be so confound at the
things going down of churches closing down
and people running here and there trying to
find somewhere to share their faith in their
god above and share his everlasting gift of
love*

By Donald Hoelscher

Bad Night

Some time in your dreams at night some wild things go through your mind like thoughts of leaving and not just out I don't know just what this means only that I do believe that the mind is always on the move and to where I don't know but I do know that some time in your sleep you can have thought's like you really can't believe

By Donald Hoelscher

Bill and Carol

*I know a couple that live on the hill they have
been so long together don't you know that
when one has to sneeze the other does so and
after all this time together in the same house
that when one has gas the other one farts I
know that this is a little farfetched but after
all of this time it's possible I guess but to stay
together for all of these years is something
else and needs to be cheered so to end this
poem I would just like to say congratulations
your well on your way*

By Donald Hoelscher

21

Blue

*When I was young if it was pink there was no
way I used to think,*

*But as I grew my thoughts did change and the
things of color really didn't matter,*

*But still there is a time for all things to be and
the time for that will come you see,*

*For I like red or maybe blue or I like yellow
how about you?*

*But still there's time when to some the color
matters at least there are some who wouldn't
rather,*

*But it seems like no matter where you go there
still are some that tell you so and they have a
preference don't you know but I am not one
to tell them so,*

By Donald Hoelscher

Blue Feelings

*Some time we get those feelings deep inside
and we try so hard for them to hide and hope
the truth is not so plain as we try to play our
silly silent game I some time wonder what to
do to keep from telling the whole real truth
that I do care there is no doubt but there is
someone who does not understand the plight
of this old lonely man oh well I guess I'll just
go on and play the game and hide my feelings
just the same instead of sharing with someone
else just another blue day that's all I'll say*

By Donald Hoelscher

Boss Lady

There is a lady from old Chicago that comes down here to run the show she has a quiet and soft spoken nature but don't rile this lady absolutely not for she can get real upset and put you in a real bad trick so I say if you want to get along do your job with nothing wrong

By Donald Hoelscher

Broke Again

Some time as we go through life we get into some awful times were we don't have a dime to spare and we don't have money to go nowhere I wish there was a magic spell to have the things we need so well but that's not the way this life will be and it's all up to you and me so we will have to do the best we can and leave it to the other man the one that holds the bag on everything that we have in dreams we think of better things and wonder when that will be

By Donald Hoelscher

Broken Love

I had a love one time I thought would always be but that's when two fools met and the biggest fool was me for I gave my heart to her and promised id always be in love with her and I would always be some time the promise that we make we cannot keep and so we go to someone else for a new love you see

By Donald Hoelscher

Busy

Did you ever have a day when life gets in your way for things you would like to do but old man time is bugging you and all those things that are in your mind will have to wait till another time I wish that I could stretch the days so time is not in my way and I could do the things I'd like to do and still have the time for me and you but life just is not that way so I guess I will need to wait till another day

By Donald Hoelscher

Can't Hide

*Why is it when we get older we wish that the
load that's on our shoulder would get much
lighter for us to handle and the distance we
carry it would get much shorter but we all
know that this ain't so and the weight and
distance just seems to grow it isn't really that
this is so but to us older ones it just seems so
and we wish there was somewhere to hide at
least for a little while*

By Donald Hoelscher

Censuses

The games up and did you hear it's time to
fess up and the dogs and cats to disappear for
just the people we will count and too get this
done there is no doubt for knocking on your
door is what we'll do to count for the roads
and the schools and make real sure we have
a voice in our congress to so we need a count
of everyone and me and you

By Donald Hoelscher

Childs Questions

Hay mommy will you tell me true when it's time to die does and angel come for you are do we just leave and go on our own to be with our God near his heavenly throne these are some questions I'd sure like to know tell me true and are these things so there is some talk that we will be in a place somewhere way out in space where we will wait for that final judgment day and be with all the others as wait to for their trip into heaven with God and the angels too

By Donald Hoelscher

Christian I Wonder

*Do I honor my God each and every day do I
help those around me with what I do and say
do I share my life with friends and family too
and how about those strangers that I see and
talk to do I greet all I meet with a friendly
hello and say nice things even when I know
there not so well let's take a look well I really
don't know I'll just do my best and hope to
pass this simple test*

By Donald Hoelscher

Christmas

*Christmas is a special time for all of us to be
of good cheer to everyone both far and near
but life to some just isn't that great we sit and
think of all our mistakes and of the past and
all we have and I guess if we think real hard
it isn't that bad*

By Donald Hoelscher

Christmas Season

The Christmas season is here alright the people are scurrying left and right the church is lit with candles bright the outside is adorned with figures bright the people are here and dressed real nice with smiles and words the world seems bright but in a world with wars and strife there's people and children here and there that don't even have some food to share their children sit in their dismal world like they do each and every year so when it's time for us to share let's remember the people over there with no food no reason for them to say it's Christmas time we'll be ok

By Donald Hoelscher

Christmas Alone

It's hard to celebrate a Christmas when your alone for the only person you have is you and the questions you have you already know the answers to so you sit and try to keep the blues from destroying what little cheer that you have mustered from going away and sliding into the feelings of dread and disappointment so the best you can do is do the best you can and roll on to another day

By Donald Hoelscher

Christmas

The Christmas season is here alright the people are scarring left and right the church is lit with candles bright the outside is adorned with figures bright the people are here and dressed real nice with smiles and words the world seems bright but in a world with wars and strife there's people and children here and there that don't even have some food to share their children sit in there dismal world like they do each and every year so when it's time for us to share let's remember the people over there with no food no reason for them to say it's Christmas well be ok

By Donald Hoelscher

Clouds

*Sometime as I look up above I think of the
people that I once loved and if there watching
us here below and what they think I wonder
so, I know if they're happy in the sky I guess so
therefore I should be, but sometimes I wonder
why it is that I am still here and of my purpose
it just isn't clear why they are gone from earth
down here and why that I am still in this
place where they once were, and I hope there
happy up there in space in the heavens that
golden place where the streets are paved with
solid gold and their waiting for us to go*

By Donald Hoelscher

Come Home Jim

It was the Easter Season and a call came from the heavens above to call some home to be with God above Jim answered the call though he knew very well that he would be missed by his family he loved but he also knew that we all have a time to leave this old world and its troubles behind so although he will be missed don't you greave for too long for someday we to will hear the same call and then we will see friends and family we love and spend our eternity with the ones up above

By Donald Hoelscher

Complain

*This morning I woke up turned on the TV just
for the news and weather to see and what they
were saying I can't understand for some are
complaining about money that's spent others
are saying come and help than railroad deaths
are on the rise with people killed but not in
cars or trucks but by people walking alone on
the rails I have not heard of many that were
deaf or blind but in this world without the
help of their family and friends for the good
Lord gave us ears to hear and eyes to see and
that's what's crazy to you me*

By Donald Hoelscher

Confused

Why do we try to live in the past when we know that it will never last dreams we had when life was good but now we don't that's understood and yet we strive to hold on tight to what was good but now is gone that isn't right so dream we do and live in the past even though it will never last and life goes on as life should do and we live on the chosen few

By Donald Hoelscher

Confusion

*My minds a jumble of thoughts and dreams
and I don't know where to begin for every day
is something new for everyone else and me and
you there are some that say the answers clear
but there just talking for someone to hear for
the jumble that's in their mind confuses them
too most of the time*

By Donald Hoelscher

Consequences

We will never know and never understand
what happens to a woman or a man one day
there strong and roaming the land the next
there sick and needing a hand I guess that's
the way this life's meant to be but me I still
don't look forward to getting that way but
I can only hope I don't end this way and go
to sleep and drift on that way to that better
place where I can hope to see the lords face
and dwell whit him there in that heavenly
place

By Donald Hoelscher

Couples

*I see couples every where they seem to have
so much to share I sit alone in this space
wondering what could have taken place to
leave me here so all alone and what I did
that was so wrong is it something I might
have said or may the place we laid our head
I sometimes wonder if it's me are was it her
and where's the love that we once shared so if
there's and answer tell me please so I can once
more try to believe and find again someone
out there who has a love that I can share.*

By Donald Hoelscher

Crazy Dream

*Last night I had a crazy dream about some
lady and me what made it really crazy was I
didn't know her we had never really met at
least I didn't think so but she got in the car
and away we did go I don't know where we
went or what we did but when we got back
to where we began she kissed me and said I
had a lovely time I hope that you did too and
maybe some time in your dreams it will once
again be me and you and we can continue
again like some old lost friends*

By Donald Hoelscher

Crazy Night

Last night as I went walking through my
mind I found some things I had one time and
dreams of things of yesterday and things that
had gone astray I wish that I could turn back
the time and be with the one I had found for
she was the love of this old man's life and to
him the best thing in this life but life the way
it is comes along and takes away the things
that we still hold dear and makes the sadness
to appear

By Donald Hoelscher

Death

I went to a wake just today and as I left the place all I could say was now they will be forever in a dreamless sleep for the rest of their eternity to weep until the Lord from above sends down his love and calls them from their graves to Heaven on high although we don't know the time or the day when they will rise from their grave and once again see the people that they once loved wives husbands or friends that were left so long in the past so now I'll close with this word of prayer I hope when I die I'll see you up there

By Donald Hoelscher

Define lonely

It's the feeling of being lost with no place to turn that is a relief of the emptiness in your mind and body it's the feeling of loss that consumes ones every thought some time it goes to the hidden recesses of your mind and stays there as a constant reminder that you are alone

By Donald Hoelscher

Describe Love

Love is it a tangible thing that can be bought or sold or is it a commodity that can be given and taken back I wonder if people realize just what love is all about to me love is not bought or sold it is freely given and both participants are bonded together by a feeling of desire to share their lives with each other and it can't be taken away true love is the love of a woman for her child or a father for his son or the desire of a man or woman to be together for life

By Donald Hoelscher

Did You Ever

Did you ever get up in a daze and wonder what day it was or go about your day and not know what you did or go for a drive and wonder how you got where you are such is the life of an old person and then you tell yourself it just a passing thing that everything will be alright in the very end

By Donald Hoelscher

Did You Ever Have

*Did you ever have a day that you really do
dread that has started early when you fell out
of bed and you feel like everything in your
body hurts and you wish that it belonged to
some other jerk but in your mind you know
what is true and the pain that you have
belongs just to you so to you the answer seems
clear so you head for the doc and pay out so
dear and it makes you wonder which hurts
the most the pain that you have or the drain
on your purse*

By Donald Hoelscher

Did You Really Ever

*I heard a story just today about a man's
indiscretions that's all I'll say or someone else
that beat a small child and didn't do nothing
for a long while to take care of the child so he
could watch the darn super bowl what kind
of world are we living in now to set everything
before what is right or what's wrong I am sure
that booze is the reason for all of these things
because it takes over our very own reason so
all I can say if booze is the reason then it's
time we stop and listen to reason for we all
know that our conscience is right and it tells
us what's wrong or what's right*

By Donald Hoelscher

Different World

Each day we get up in a different world if you don't believe it just look around the grass has grown the trees are in bloom the flowers have opened and the day of the week have changed to another day oh well we are told to live like each day is our last so with that in mind welcome to a brand new world

By Donald Hoelscher

Do You Ever

*Have you ever thought of being young again
so you could do what you did back then and
do and say just what you want and never
worry about things like they were some big
joke but we know that life don't work that
way and our time of young has gone away
Like the flowers on a winters day so I guess
the things for us to do is take the time that's
given you and make the best of everyday and
live our lives while we're here ok*

By Donald Hoelscher

Do You Ever Wonder

Did you ever wonder whether something is wrong or right and sit there a thinking it's a heck of a plight it seems the more that you ponder the worse it seems to get until you worked yourself into a terrible fit of what is wrong or maybe is right and still you ponder all through the night and wake up still all bent out of shape and still the problem just seems to remain but to get rid of it is sure the darn pits and I wonder in my feeble little mind if this is what's going to happen all of the time

By Donald Hoelscher

Don't Blink

When life's going your way don't blink for life can change in that instant

When you going down the road on a narrow drive don't blink for you can end up in a ditch

If you're watching a toddler don't blink for in that small amount of time they can get into any thing

When you're getting older and life is getting short don't blink for in that time you could be on your way to a better place

So try to live life with both eyes open and try hard not to blink

By Donald Hoelscher

Don't Be Afraid

*When I was young and went to bed my parents
always told me don't worry you will be alright
just go to sleep and turn out the light close
your eyes and ease your mind tomorrow is
another day then you can get up to run and
play when you grow up and have kids of your
own then it's different and you'll understand
why there is no longer reason to be afraid*

By Donald Hoelscher

Don't Be Sure

*They say that we can only be sure of what
we see I say don't be too sure as the eyes fool
us into believing that the world around us
is safe well wake up there are people being
killed robbed, and hurt, by people, cars,
trucks, airplanes, war, and by people so I
say be on guard for the people you meet treat
everyone as a potential threat don't be too
sure remember the only thing certain is that
nothing is certain*

Donald Hoelscher

Don't Blink

*When we're born we are alone in our thoughts
except for mom and dad we are alone then we
grow up and things start to change and the
things we saw as a child that didn't matter
now for awhile seem to be just the now thing
and the things that were so peaceful and quiet
now just don't seem right and the me and you
of yesterday is not what we are today so in the
time from when we were small in the blink
of an eye we have progressed into a different
person with new ideas and thoughts for our
tomorrow*

By Donald Hoelscher

Don't Bug Me

*Don't tell me this is wrong or I am not where
I belong or I am not welcome come here are
there or if I am not dressed to be in here the
lord made me just like you and he made me
in all colors too but the main thing that I
would like to say is I am not ever in your way
I may not be dressed in a suit or in a dinner
gown but in my mind I still belong and one
thing is for sure I am just like you because the
God above still loves me too*

By Donald Hoelscher

Don't Crash Computer

I had a small problem with my computer today
so I thought I'd be smart and start again but
had I known the problems I'd have there is no
way I would have started this whole bunch of
bull well you get the message and I guess it's
ok and I have succeeded in some sort of way
the thing is running and limping along but
this is enough for now I am gone

By Donald Hoelscher

Don't Drive Walk

*As of now the word is out that people
everywhere are piggin out and what they
carry is a sight and there isn't any where
to hide and is there for all to see and that
includes both you and me so I guess what I
am trying to say is there must be a better way
so no more fast food or candy snacks so when
we go shopping just put it back and so there is
two things we will do and that is to lose that
old middle inner tube so if its close its best to
walk and loose some of that excess bulk*

By Donald Hoelscher

Don't Judge Me

*Because I don't always agree with you don't
mean that I am wrong and because you don't
agree with me don't mean that you are wrong
so don't expect me to always agree with you
or bow down to your way the first rule to
getting along is to   learn to respect yourself
and if you can't respect yourself how can you
also respect me too or the ones around you age
doesn't always denote maturity or that the
lack of common sense is based on age*

By Donald Hoelscher

Don't Tempt Fate

*In this world there are lots of folks who live
on dreams and schemas of things they hear
about are things from their dreams I believe
that were all subject to all these foolish things
but to act upon these things and dreams is
what makes us the people that we are and
helps us to fly today and ride there in a car
so I for one will listen to my dreams and act
upon the foolish schemas for you really never
know what else there is to do and the next
great invention may come from me are you*

By Donald Hoelscher

Don't Worry Love

In sleep the other night it seem like I was up all night but I know that can't be true for some time in the night I made love to you and as I held you tight and I wished the time would always last but then the reality once more set in and you were gone once again it seems that life is always there to kill the time we have to share

By Donald Hoelscher

Dread

Are you lonely let's take a look and see do
you look at couples and wish that they were
me and sit at home staring out to see if some
ones going to come and visit this time of day
are do you feel alone and wonder what to do
and listen for the phone waiting for someone
to call and talk to you I still don't understand
why this had to be that I am all alone and
there are couples all around you see I don't
know the answer but I sure wish I did than
those feelings wouldn't be running in my
head

By Donald Hoelscher

Dream of Home

Last night as I slept in a long dream filled slumber the Lord came to visit me in my sleep he told me that soon he would be calling me home to be with him in his heavenly home I said Lord please not yet and I began to cry there are so many things I have yet to try he just smiled at me and told me it would soon be my time to leave this old world and all behind and join him in the big blue sky of the heavens above where I would join again the ones I once loved down here in this world so I guess to end this poem I would just have to say when it's our time well just go away to be with our God and his son in their heavenly home in the sky

By Donald Hoelscher

Dream World

In a dream world everything is fine and what we wish we get all the time but in this world we live in today that's not the case I have to say so all we can do is do our best and rely on parents to do the rest for we know they will be for us always there for we know that they will always care for no matter what we do they will be there to see us through .

By Donald Hoelscher

Dreams

I had a dream one time of places
I would go, if I but had the chance
And the where with all to go but
dreams are just fleeting things and
And I guess that's rightly so for if they were
a tangible things we'd all be sure to go So
I guess we can live in dreams and hope
someday it's so

By Donald Hoelscher

Each Night

Every night as I walk in the door I am filled with a sense of foreboding lore of things that were here in the past and a feeling of why they didn't last and if it's me who is to blame or someone else I shall not name oh well I'll just have to sit and stew and always wonder if it's you and why I am still here so all alone and no one around with me to share this home

By Donald Hoelscher

Early Late

It was Tuesday morning it was almost time to go and it seemed like my giddy up was awfully slow it seems like the time was flying right by and when I looked at the clock I saw the reason why for that few minutes of rest I thought was such a treat had turned into an hour so now don't you know the panic set in and it was hurry lets go the bus will be here and don't move so slow and finally the kids are ready we will make it this time but next time I'll leave them few minutes behind

By Donald Hoelscher

Easter Day

*It's Easter morning the kids are up and the
Easter bunny has already done his stuff now
it's time and the race has begun to get ready
for church and hope that it won't start early
this year the priest is there in the robes of the
season than church has started and wouldn't
you know one the kids is putting on a show
and as we say something the kid starts to bawl
and it seems the whole church is taking it all
in oh well such is the life of a parent again*

By Donald Hoelscher

Empty House

*Why is it when we're alone a house seems
to take on different sounds of their own
like creaks and pops up into the night and
shadows and things that don't seem right and
dreams of things long in the past that seems
to be real at least while they last I guess what
I am trying to say is an empty house is not
the way*

By Donald Hoelscher

Exasperation

Is there ever a time when there's things to do and no matter how hard you try to work it through it seems like nothing's going to change for you so in a fit of total duress you walk away and do your best to try to hold on to your cool but somewhere in your mind you know the answers there but like a ghost you cannot see it lingers there inside you see

By Donald Hoelscher

Eyes of a Child

It would be nice to see the world through the eyes of a child and see only good and love in this world but that's not the way this life seems to go with stories of wars and killings galore sometime it seems like the theme of this place is hate and discontent all over the world some day we hope at least in our time we'll see peace and love and call each other friend

By Donald Hoelscher

Faded Love

*If a love is given and not returned how do you
go forward and not be burned or avoid the
pain that is coming in the end what prompts
us to continue on the same path even though
we know that it is not going to last or dream
about what happened a while ago and live in
the past that we know will never be and bask
in our own form of misery I don't know the
answer but I really hope so to someday have
the answer at least I hope so*

By Donald Hoelscher

Fair Weather Friend

I had someone one time I thought was a good friend of mine but I found out the other day and where I stood was far away so I made up my mind today to leave this person so far away and not go back no more again and leave her with her part time friend it seems the green eyed monster is there and he don't like for her time to share

By Donald Hoelscher

Father Dave

There is man that I know who every Sunday tells us so and from the bible he does read the way to live if we believe what to say and not to do and how we should live if were to do what is always right in Gods sight so with some insight from the priest and on our knees like we believe that God is present in this place and at this service we call a mass were from his hands we receive again once more the Lord above. and as we venture from this place we remember what has taken place that God has come into our mists to bless us now for another week

By Donald Hoelscher

Father's Day

There is a time every year when all the family gathers near to honor someone that's in there mists that has tried real hard to meet the test, to raise a family for the best and though some time he stumbled there he never failed to show he cared and when the time is here for him to go I am sure his family will always know so as we honor our fathers both gone and here be sure to show them that you still care

By Donald Hoelscher

Feelings

There is a place inside our hearts that stores our feelings and our thoughts it leaves no place for the mistakes we make and reminds us of our thoughts and misgivings this constant reminder drives us mad with dreams of what we should have had .and probably will most every day until at last. we all go away, to that great place somewhere above the place were told we will go with all our friends that left so long ago and I believe. and they tell me so and once again the heart will know and tell us what we all should do and the path that we should follow through

By Donald Hoelscher

Friend

Sometime we find a friend down here some one- we could hold so dear. Some one that to us would always share our life our lows and all our cares to be with us throughout our life to be to us a loving wife, a friend to be with us through thick and thin. To be with us until the end

By Donald Hoelscher

Fired No Quit Yes

If kids can get away with the things they do and say and run and tell things that are not true today I shudder to think of the future and when they get on their own who will they run to when there not at home Life will teach them a lessen and this you best believe for the ones you step on now are the ones that will have their say There are times in this life when we step on some ones toes and think it's quite ok But you had best believe that there will come a day when you will have to pay

By Donald Hoelscher

First Love

I had a girl one time I thought to make my wife for I had often told her she was the love of my life and so one day the time did come to ask her the big question if she agree to be instead of two just be me and you she ask me what had took so long for me to pop the question and I told her I was not sure the answer I would get and so I waited until I was sure of what the answered be so now you know the story and how its sure to be so now there's no I it's now just you and me

By Donald Hoelscher

Fish

Today as I sat there by the phone it began to ring don't you know a very good friend did invite me up to eat and I'll have to say it was quite a treat because the thought of some soup and cheese was not high on my list you best believe so I headed on up the hill and enjoyed myself a very good meal so all I can say is thank you for a very good feed and is very appreciated you best believe

By Donald Hoelscher

Flying High

*Did you ever wish that you could fly and sour
like the birds way up in the sky and live like
the birds wild and free and not be troubled
like you and me in the dream I built a plane
that you would peddle to where you began
and start to live the way that you once began
and be at peace and harmony with the world
here on earth and get along with others in the
world of your birth but this is just a dream
but how I wish it was so but this just will not
happen and you can bet that this is so*

By Donald Hoelscher

Foolish Questions

Some time when this life goose the other way what to do or what to say becomes the question in our minds and what to do is a silly question and though we ponder this every day we find in the end there is no way so we find that what we have found is not the way and there is not and answer so we have to say oh well tomorrow is just another day

By Donald Hoelscher

For Kathy

Going Home to see my friends who have passed away and waiting to greet me in the heavens today I know I'll be missed I am sorry to say but my God has called me so I am on my way so please don't be sad not after today for ill be in heaven with the lord on this day so goodbye to my family my husband my children parents and friends and all of you gathered to see me on my way to heaven today

By Donald Hoelscher

Forever Blue

If I could turn back the clock and change the things that now are not I wonder what I'd do to change the heart ache I am going through and stop this pain I live with day by day and just make this pain just go away but I don't see how to make the change and all I say most every day is that someday it will go away maybe I will find someone that will be to me the only one and be my love till life is through and be to me just me and you

By Donald Hoelscher

Friend

Sometime we find a friend down here someone we could hold so dear someone that to us would always share our life and all our cares to be with us throughout our life to be to us a loving spouse a friend to be with us through thick and thin to be with us until the end

By Donald Hoelscher

Frustration

*In this space of thoughts and schemes there
is a place for all our dreams and things that
we do not plan seem to get so out of hand like
a simple thing like fix a car that we think
will only take a while or when you are in a
hurry there is someone that makes us worry
about the things we need to do or keeps us
from what we need to do so I guess what I am
trying to say is keep your cool along the way
and don't be frustrated that's all I'll say*

By Donald Hoelscher

Getting Feeble

Getting old is sure the pits and the older you get the more life just seems to change with each passing day and when you talk you run out of things to say for the thoughts you had just seem to fade like the snow on a sunny day but still there is a time when you do or say some crazy things that have gone away and what you meant to do or say like the weather they too have long gone away

By Donald Hoelscher

Getting Old

There once was a time when everything worked
and to get around quick wasn't a joke but now
that's all changed and I hobble around and
look for something to really hold on a hand
rail a shopping basket or something like that
it don't really matter as long as its strong and
holds this old body as I hobble along there are
those who say it's all just and act but there
not the ones with the pain in their back so all
I can say is their time will come when they
like me will also hobble around

By Donald Hoelscher

Getting Older

*As the time here just seems to pass and one
day we look around and ask what happened
to the man I used to be and who is this old
person in the mirror I see is this someone that
I once knew or some stranger I am talking
to and why does this person look so old and
wonder around so dog gone slow could this
person that I see be just the one and only me*

By Donald Hoelscher

Gloom

*I met this lady just today she seemed so sad I
have to say I read her a poem and she did cry
and big old tears flowed from her eyes I ask
her if she was alright and she said yes to my
delight and so I read her a few more poems
and she did smile for awhile so I guess the
way to end this poem was a big hug before I
am gone and I'll send you some if you won't
cry so as for now I'll say goodbye*

By Donald Hoelscher

Gloomy Day

I stumble on from day to day and hope that things will change but the only thing I see so far is a lot more of the same so if in this life there is only strife and pain then why go on and try at all if there is nothing left to gain but then I see kids playing and running all around and parents pulling out there hair and screaming at their child and know that life isn't so bad and I can still smile remembering that my kids are gone and have been for a while

By Donald Hoelscher

God is Love

Sometime I think of God above and what he's given to us is love and of the times that I forgot the reason I'm here is to give my love and as I ponder of all these things above I wonder if I have given all my love for each of us has a reason to be down here and that's a given to share Gods love to everyone and to all that Gods people sent from above I know there is no way to even to get close to what Gods given to each of us we each have a purpose and that's a fact whether we realize it or push it back there is no way to even get close to what Gods given in his love for each of us for the love he has there is no measure and to each of us that is our treasure

By Donald Hoelscher

God is Real

There are those of them that think that God is real and those that think that that isn't so but me I know that if he isn't then we're all fools and that's a given so try as we might to prove he is we still fall short and that's a fact we can try to pretend that this isn't so and live our lives in a dream land world but me I know that God is real for when I fail my mind does say you know you're wrong and try again to be strong for with his help we do no wrong and if we fail he's still right there to say ok I understand that you'll make mistakes along the way and I'll forgive and guide the way to that place where we belong on heavenly home by Gods throne

By Donald Hoelscher

Going Home

My time on earth is at and end And I must leave my wife, kids, And friends, to work no more Down here below to leave this Place and all its show, and as I Leave I want all to know, that I will miss them, the ones I love So, now don't you greave and Take it slow for your time will Come for down below I know The lord will see me through As I wait, in heaven for all of YOU!!

By Donald Hoelscher

Gone

*The seasons change and so do we just look
around and you will see the people that we
once knew are going each day as the years
pass by so now is the time to reap and sew
he thinks it's time to enjoy the show of times
of good and times of bad and enjoy the good
times we have had because someday soon we'll
be like them and be at rest forever more*

By Donald Hoelscher

Good

*Did you ever have a night when everything
was not right and you toss and turn and at
last you finally go to sleep to be woke up soon
by that alarm's study beep some time I just
don't know just what to think and so tonight
I'll try again to beat this lack of sleep again*

By Donald Hoelscher

Goodbye

*There is one thing in this world of ours the
makes us sad it's the long goodbye it seems
that when somebody leaves it leaves us home
for us to grieve for we don't know when they
will be back are again the time that it will
last*

By Donald Hoelscher

Good Morning Missouri

Well it's Monday the beginning of another long week and I am so tired and need some more sleep but a caption I once heard says there is no rest for the wicked and I never realized I was so bad but I guess since I am I'll do the best I can and go along with the flow and keep on keeping on that's the way to go so if you're in the same old boat my advice to you is with your chin up and your hand on your billfold be real careful of which way you go 'cause there is always someone out there with their hand sticking out looking for some of your money to help them back out

By Donald Hoelscher

Good Morning World

*As I opened my eyes and realized that I was
still here on this earth I thanked my God for
one more day and said to myself there is still
a way to change this life that has gone astray
and do the things to change my way and make
my life more to the pattern that is Gods way I
don't really know the answers but still I wish
I knew what my God still wants me to do and
ill still listen to my heart and hope it's true or
what my God wants me to do*

By Donald Hoelscher

Government Reps

*I believe that if it's for the people the ones we
have elected seem to frown on anything that
is for the people it seems that when the United
States was founded that it was based on the
principal of by the people for the people but
if you will listen to our representatives in
office that we have elected they have forgot
the reason they were elected while they're
living high on the hog the other half are losing
jobs, homes, and living day by day folks who
have served this USA are being denied the
compensation that they were promised after
twenty years they have worked for because
of some more of their messed up judgment
they seem to resist any thing that will give the
ordinary folks a hand up they have forgotten
where the money they live on comes from
or the reason they are elected my hats off to
anyone that would stand up for the ordinary
folks and their plight*

By Donald Hoelscher

Grouch and Grump

We get up in the morning and rush all around but we don't feel the part and each thing seems to confound the kids won't help and the cat can't be found and the dog is excited and barking at each sound well some days it don't seem to matter because before we get ready were already madder the cats finally found the dog is put out and the kids are now ready and running about with where is my lunch I can't find my book and all you can say is did you really look then at last we're ready and head out the door and we have been called a grouch and a grump once more

By Donald Hoelscher

Grown Up

*As we grow up and we mature the things of
our child hood disappear The strife of life
soon fills our lives and soon the hopes and
dreams are there And still our lives are filled
with fear that we will fail at what we do and
we will have trouble being me or you So to
this life I'll tell you true there is someone to
help and guide through For he has told 'us
he'll be there and help us find our life to share
if we will just believe he's there*

By Donald Hoelscher

Happy Valentine's Day

There is someone in our life that makes a person feel alive they are the object of our love and make us feel like we belong they enter in our dreams at night and make us feel oh so right so to those of us that have a love I say always try to do what's right and hold her tight every night

By Donald Hoelscher

Hard Goodbye

*Did you ever feel like you don't know what
you're going to do and every road you want
to take seems to be the wrong one at least
according to everyone you see I wish that I
could change the life I have been living but as
of yet have not have been able to break this
tie and I don't know if this feeling will ever
leave me with the peace of mind to go on to
someone else this is the hell you go through
when you care too much*

By Donald Hoelscher

Hard Night

*Last night as I tried to sleep thoughts of work
and things kept me awake as I rolled and
tossed my mind was a blaze of the things in
my mind of yesterday I hope that tonight is
better for me for working all night just don't
quite agree some time I wonder but really
don't know what's in the cards when the cards
are dealt out to you and me I guess all we can
do is wait and see and it isn't up to you and
me*

By Donald Hoelscher

Have You

*Have you ever driven down a long lonely road
and thought of your past and things that never
should be told and thought of your future and
things of the past of people and places and
what didn't last some time I wonder what
life's all about and just when I think I have it
all figured out something happens to turn my
world all about so here I go again stumbling
about and once more wondering what my
life's all about*

By Donald Hoelscher

Have You Ever

*Did you ever have a day so long that no
matter what you do or say there is not any
way to change the things that come your way
and though you try and do your best there is
no way to meet the test and you stumble and
fret and worry still there is no way to duck
the bills and so you do the best you can your
still in bills all along and worry and as your
hair turns gray you have already realized
there is no way*

By Donald Hoelscher

Heartaches

I woke up this morning with no way to cure this pain I have inside some people claim it's the empty house feeling I think it's more of the empty heart feeling the fact that you're alone and the prospect of being alone for weeks on end has finally got to the point where it's becoming too much for me to tolerate much longer I am going to start looking for someone who is alone like me to be with it seems that the love I have for the woman in my life now is not even cared about and when I tell her I love her she is cold and can't even say the same to me which leaves me to believe that I am just a tool to get what she needs

By Donald Hoelscher

Hey! It's TGIF

We have waited all week long for this very day and look forward to tomorrow for in our bed to stay and get some extra rest so next week to meet the test of another very long old week and Mondays tough they say Tuesday we do a little better Wednesday we're on our way Thursday we start to slow way down and then it's Friday what else can you say Saturday there's things to do we have put off all week long Sunday its go to church then we start again

By Donald Hoelscher

Hey Mom

*Did you ever see to fail when you first get up in
the morning the kids are always in rare form
and no matter the temp its mom I am cold
or where is my favorite shirt or did you do
the wash and when are we leaving you know
I can't be late and so you get half dressed get
the kids to school and hurry back home to get
yourself ready to just another day hay mom*

By Donald Hoelscher

Hidden Feelings

Hi it's me and don't you know that I am here and now you know so please don't leave me here alone like this and act like you really care just to use me everywhere I have feelings don't you know even if you don't think so if you too have some too then tell me now I beg of you

By Donald Hoelscher

Hold On Tight

*I had a dream up into the night about someone
to hold me tight and be with me for a while
and give to me again that warm sweet smile
to hold me when I need a friend and be with
me until the end but dreams now is all I have
to comfort me in the night and memories are
always there to hold me tight and assure me
and tell me I am all right it's said that no
man is an island now I know that's sure right
for we all need someone to hold us at least
some nights*

By Donald Hoelscher

Home for Sale

After many years of living in this house I call home I have decided to sell this house I called home for thirty some out years and retire to a smaller place I will leave many memories behind both good and bad but like the song says it's time to move along and find happiness somewhere else so if you're interested in a well used home with lots of memories there are three bed rooms up and one down below two full baths ready to go so if you need more info just let me know

By Donald Hoelscher

Homework Blues

*Today I watched a little girl doing the things
for today she wasn't very happy this I'll have
to say for there was a million things she
would rather do or say and you can bet it
wasn't homework this I sure can say for this
thing that was homework can't Be done today
for she had a million things she rather do
today but, some time before tomorrow this
I sure can say there will come a time when
homework is done today*

By Donald Hoelscher

Hope

*Some time we feel like it's the end then we
find someone called friend and linger with
them awhile and share their laughter and
there smiles and then we stumble on once
more to be alone in some old place where we
can stare out there in vacant space so I guess
the way to end this poem is not to be out there
alone and remember that our god is near to
help us through our hopes and fears*

By Donald Hoelscher

How Can

Why is it that someone you once loved can
turn so cold like the clouds above and act like
they no longer care and leave you feeling oh
so bare like the trees in the fall outside and
be so cold like winter wind that cuts right
through your heart again the answer now I
wish I knew so I could start somewhere a new
and be the person that I once was and have
again someone to love

By Donald Hoelscher

How Do You Spell Lonely

Is it something that you feel or is it something you think was real can it be a person that you met or someone that you can't forget or maybe it's a feeling that you have about something that's gone bad I wish the answer was in black and white than it wouldn't torture us through the night and make us realize what were not and make us sad an sorry for what we haven't got

By Donald Hoelscher

How Many

*How many times in this life do we wish that
we had a husband are a wife and a place to
lay our head that we could do without the
dread of worrying about the wolf at the door
are any other things that's for sure I don't
think there will ever be a day when at least to
me that I can say I am fine no more worries at
least today but I think when they finally lay
me down I will no longer be worry bound*

By Donald Hoelscher

How To

*As I lay here in this bed I feel my mind fill
in with dread and wonder where this feeling
goes   when we go to sleep at night I really
kind of wish I knew than I could duck these
morning blues and this nagging feeling of
what is the blasé and hide the feelings in my
eyes for it's said that the eyes are the windows
of the soul if this is true than I am so busted
now you know and I can't hide these feelings
of those blues*

By Donald Hoelscher

How to survive camp

When we signed up it looked ok and we all
looked forward to a nice stay, but then the
time came, for us to go and then reality of
camp begin to show to go to bed when the
time was right and not to watch the TV all
night with all our shows well be sure to miss
and the parents with their sweet good night
kiss and a pat to say it will be alright. and to
go to sleep I'll see you later when you wake up
it will all be better and think about the days
ahead and all the fun that we will have the
time together with all these good friends .

By Donald Hoelscher

Human Weakness

*Some time when were alone we think of the
things that went wrong and wonder why this
had to be and why it happened to you and me
I don't really know the answer so to someone
else I will have to go he is not of this here place
but somewhere out there in space but he has
told us long ago that he is always there you
know so when things go up in smoke just be
aware that he is there and he has told us that
he cares*

By Donald Hoelscher

Humility

Take a walk in humility am I a good person let's take a look and see do I respect my parents do I respect my elders do I care for the people below my stature am I a responsible individual in my community am I the one who stands up for the feelings of other people my teachers law enforcement strangers on the street homeless and those who have nothing neglected kids as well am I a good neighbor a good father or mother a good son or a daughter but most of all am I a decent human being

By Donald Hoelscher

Hungry

We get up in the morning we want something to eat and then we do and we become hungry again not for food but things that we need and we do what we have to and get what we can than like before were hungry again so once more the cycle begins again and we start all over just like before only now the hunger has grown so strong that simple things that we get are now never enough

By Donald Hoelscher

Hurry up We're Late

*It's Sunday morning the alarm wasn't set so
once more we're going to be late so we can
chalk it up again to a goofy mistake oh well
we'll just have to do the best that we can and
hope we don't meet up with that preacher
man I really don't look forward to a lecture
today and I can envision just what he will
say so with any luck we'll slip in again and
sit down before the service begins*

By Donald Hoelscher

I am

*There are those that say they are a Christian
but I see what they do each day just don't
really show them as a Christian they do
what they want and treat each other bad
and when Sunday comes they are on their
way but when they get to church don't you
know they complain about where they have
to park once again*

By Donald Hoelscher

I Am Fat

*Did you ever wonder what other folks think
of you if you think your fat what in the world
must other people think of me or you as for
me I really don't know though it really doesn't
matter I'll tell you true it's not what they
think it's all up to you there are books written
and to me I don't care I am very happy with
all of me there*

By Donald Hoelscher

I Am He

We have a Father up above that showers us every day with his love He guides us on our way if we will listen to what he says But like the children that we have we don't always hear the words that he has said And wander on our merry way so like the Father that he is he takes us back and forgives So when you wander from the path remember he will always bring you back and dry the tears that you have cried and heal your hurts the ones inside

By Donald Hoelscher

I Believe

God put us down here to accomplish a certain number of things but to most of us were so far behind that we will never die so we struggle with the burdens of work kids and everyday life so to all of us poor slobs that struggle day by day I say remember to take time to smell the roses and when possible spend a day to ourselves remember the sanity you save might be your own and none of us has more than one to lose sanity is what keeps us from being total idiots

By Donald Hoelscher

I Can't

*If I was a betting man I say this country is in
the pan and were all in a hell of a fix with all
the crap that's left to fix if everything that's
wrong was right we could sleep well at night
but seeing things as they are were and   like
the pig that gave its all were in the pan I hear
the promises that are made to fix this world
and stop these things but like the stuff that
they put out all we see is a lot more mouth I'd
like to hear someone say we have to stop this
isn't the way*

By Donald Hoelscher

I Believe

I believe there is a Santa and we can see him just walking around he isn't in red and doesn't ride in a sleigh and don't have any reindeer to guide him on his way and he isn't always in a red suit but he's still around and where there is laughter he's sure to be found although some time we can't see it the thought is still there and if we but look and we don't have to stare we'll find him standing at home or on the street be nice for he could be someone you meet

By Donald Hoelscher

I Knew

I knew someone one time that reminded them of me and the life I had with the love I had for me, there wasn't one thing I could do that they didn't disagree and for me to speak or visit with someone of the other sex was never for me to be well although I loved the other one and couldn't quite believe that to be so possessive put me on a constant watch and dishonest I had to be

By Donald Hoelscher

I Look Out

*As I look out at the new fallen snow it occurs
again to me that we really don't know how
this miracle to us is done all we can think is
there is work to be done so with shovels and
blades we trek on out and clear the paths so
we can walk about and not be worried about
a broken arm leg are a hip you know that's
a terrible thing so let's go to work with our
tools again to clean up this side walk so we
can walk again*

By Donald Hoelscher

I Saw

I was looking at the computer screen and I saw someone a long lost friend and uncle that I once had that now is gone and makes me sad some time when we look around we find things that bring us down to long lost people of our past and a life for them that did not last I wonder if someday we'll see them in our time the ones that for now are so long gone

By Donald Hoelscher

I Wish

There are times in this life when we wish we could rewind our life and change the things in our past to make us happy in our lives at last but rewind this life is not to be so we'll just have to let things be its bad but what else can we do but do what we have to do so if in this place of time down here we will just live and let be

By Donald Hoelscher

I wish I Knew

*Did you ever find yourself in a predicament
where you don't know where to go or what to
do are for that matter how to do what you
know you should do and the more you try to
do what's right the more confused you become
and confusion becomes your friend and all
you can think about is the total helpless and
the thoughts of just saying the heck with it
and just give up and put your head in the
sand like some ostrich*

By Donald Hoelscher

I Wonder

*Some time I wonder why I am here and a
thought comes in my mind that I am just here
to spend some time to see if I can find the
truth of what I am and why I am here my life
has some time been the pits and some time I
just want to split and go to a place where I
can belong with someone who to is lost and
then I wonder if it's really worth the cost*

By Donald Hoelscher

If

If birds can mate for all their life why can't
people do the like we change our minds and
stray apart and break apart each other's
heart to stray again to someone else to start
to build something else we think is true and
even though we act real happy the bottom line
is pretty crappy for like the end of our first
love we get real tired of our new love and
when the time grows to the end we wonder
once more how to end so we stay apart and
act real busy and live a life so well apart and
try not to once more break another heart

By Donald Hoelscher

If I Could Change

*If I could change what would I do how could
I start my life anew and mend the heart's I
know I've broken and take back all the lies I
have spoken and start again to mend my life
and be faithful to my loving wife and show
her that she's the one and start again to build
the love I thought I lost again be a loving and
faithful friend*

By Donald Hoelscher

I'll Tell

*I'll tell you now and here's the thing that love
is what makes our old bell ring and make us
do some silly things like chase a girl and buy
a ring and then the trouble does really start
and it isn't long before our life begins with
kids around and all those things so I guess
that all I can say is if love isn't here it's on the
way so if you think that this isn't right just try
looking left or right*

By Donald Hoelscher

Imagine

Imagine if you can a life with no end with unending happiness no sorrow within some time in my mind I try to pretend that this life just a stepping stone or just a beginning with no end its said that we are just here for a while and then we will pass away with a smile to a place where happiness is the mode in our life's with no more sorrow or no more trials

By Donald Hoelscher

In Dreams

Sometime when I sleep at night someone goes walking through my mind and every day as I wake anew I look hopefully for that dream to come true and as I stumble through the day I look around and hope and pray for the one I dream about will sometime soon come walking out

By Donald Hoelscher

In My Dreams

*In my dreams at night I long to hold you oh so
tight and love you all night long at least until
till the break of dawn but dreams is all that I
still have and a dream is just a fleeting thing
that comes and goes just like the spring when
flowers and trees all do bud and in the fall
they lose their stuff so like the trees of nature
go so do we and wait for snow when like the
cold in winter time as we grow old this is
what we find*

By Donald Hoelscher

Indecisive

*It seems like when we get older simple
decisions get even bolder like what to wear
how to dress when to lay down to rest bills
to pay well there is always another day and
then the one that makes us shutter to move or
not it's such a bother you wait for something
good to happen and then it does and you say
ok now it's come is it ok should I do what I
said or should I pass right now instead*

By Donald Hoelscher

Isn't It Funny

Don't it seem funny that love kindness and
forgiveness are so soon forgotten and words
of anger are always remembered it seems like
forever I wish there was a way to recall every
angry word and thought given in the past and
replace them with words of kindness love and
compassion but needless to say words spoken
in anger don't seem to ever go away and they
seem to be forever encased in the place in our
minds that we can't seem to reach

By Donald Hoelscher

Ain't Friday Yet

*I got up this morning my eyes won't stay open
did you ever have a day when everything's
slow no matter how hard you try nothing will
go and you stager along trying to get ready
but your eyes won't stay open and needless
to say this is bound to be a miserable day
so you do the best that you can and say to
yourself my this is going to be one hell of a
day I have things to do and don't you know
bed will come to soon this is one thing I know
I'm Just Tired*

By Donald Hoelscher

Its Friday

Its Friday the day we have all been looking for at least four days we had hump day but now the long awaited day is here now we are waiting for time to go home than we have a sat a sun day but we also have a Monday time to enjoy the bed for and extra hour or two if the parents are willing to leave us be we can only hope this is so me too we are all kids at heart when it comes to time off

By Donald Hoelscher

It's Funny

*Isn't it funny when someone is on your mind
and you know they have a problem and you
want to help so you get on the phone and
rattle the cage of someone you know needs
help with their problem and the thoughts of
helping is so strong on your mind that you
wake up early and get out of bed and call
them on the phone to ask them what will it
take to fix what's wrong*

By Donald Hoelscher

Jealousy

*There is something you can't see that follows
around you and me and makes our lives so
miserable you see it's not something you can
touch see are pick it up, there are folks that
call it the green monster and sometime it can
follow us around and drive us right out of
our mind with feelings that are so strong it
seems that we don't know what to do and all
we want is to be with the one we care about
and in this case it's him and you*

By Donald Hoelscher

Just

*How do you spell lonely is it a feeling you
get in your mind or the fact that your alone
almost all of the time I really don't know as
of today but if I was to guess I would surely
say it's a feeling that comes from inside of our
heart that has all the power to tear us apart
and make us do things we would not normally
do and leave us real sad and awfully blue so
enough of this old pity party stuff to get past
this feeling you need to get tough*

By Donald Hoelscher

Just a Friend

When you know someone for many years and then one day you finally hear that they have gone to their final rest and you wonder why like all the rest but in your mind you already know in our time we have to go to meet our master in the heavens above for he has called them to share his mercy and his love

By Donald Hoelscher

Just a Thought

If there was a dream you would be in it if there was a place you would be there if it was a thought it would be you if it were happiness it would be us just be me and you

By Donald Hoelscher

Just an Old Fool

*I sit here wondering what to do to pass the
time and not be blue
my mind tells me theirs things to do my body
tell me what's wrong with you if you listen
to your mind you will pay for it are or you
blind but as the discussions go on in my mind
the clock says get up now it's already past the
time so once more I stumble from my bed to
face the long old day ahead I get up finally
splash some water on my face get myself busy
picking up the place you never know who
could be by*

By Donald Hoelscher

Just Asleep

*As I lay here in my bed with thoughts a
running through my head of things I had here
in the past and friends I had that didn't last
and as I wondered in my dream of things I
heard and places I had seen and I wondered
if this was a dream of what was real of what
I had seen some time I really just don't know
or why the dreams do trouble so or if the
answer is in my mind of sad old places and
troubled times*

By Donald Hoelscher

Just Don't Know

*When I was a child my parents would say
just be patient it will all go away but to me
this thinking is getting awfully old, kind of
like this old man I am told but it's also said
that it will surely get better in time but I am
still hoping it's true at least all the time what
I need now is a friend for the rest of my life
and if possible a sweet loving wife it is said
that love springs eternal I hope this is so for
the way things are going it sure is so slow*

By Donald Hoelscher

Just for Fun

There is a lady that I met that I really can't forget although I met her just one time her picture seems to stand out in my mind like some old forgotten place that is somewhere out there in outer space but still my mind tells me that I should find and tell her that she has a place in my mind not somewhere out there in another space and time and if I could arrange this space and time she would not just be on my mind but in my arms at least some time

By Donald Hoelscher

Just Life

*Last night as I sat here in this house I wondered
what was wrong or right about the things we
do or say and why people act this way is it
something in there genes and is it just that
they are mean in what they do and say or
maybe it's just there ignorant ways some time
I can relate to this and then again sometime I
just can't understand the difference between
a woman and a man*

By Donald Hoelscher

Just Lonely

When you wake up in the morning with a
pain that can't be taken away with a ill and it
seems to be centered around the part of your
body that keeps you alive but is easily broken
and can be given away or at least the feelings
in the heart and it becomes a constant hurt
and pain that becomes completely and totally
unbearable what do you do to ease the pain
or cure the ache that seems to remain very
much a part of you

By Donald Hoelscher

Just Old

*I think about my younger days when I could
run around and play and that's not what it is
today for now I am now old and gray and no
longer able to fool around and play that's not
to say I am ready yet for the grave for even old
folks have their place even though they can't
win a race there knowledge makes then very
handy in a pinch so you best think real heard
before you throw them away for you might
need them again some day*

By Donald Hoelscher

Just Old Folks

I went to and anniversary just yesterday there
I met some lady's and I would have to say I
had a nice visit and the food it was great but
like me once more I did over eat so the result
will be ill carry it around for a while and
grumble and groan about every darn pound
so about all of this id just have to say all in
all it was a nice day

By Donald Hoelscher

Just Poor

*Every day you see the news of heartbreak by
some poor fool And as you think of their sad
plight you wonder if this is wrong or right
well I am not sure what the answer is but as
for me I quite agree that some time we all
must pay and look our self's for a better way
we can't be all born with a silver spoon so
us poor folks that struggle on must somehow
find a better way since we don't have that
silver spoon though we work hard from day
to day there just don't seem to be no way*

By Donald Hoelscher

Just Resting

*I talked to a man just the other day and
listened carefully to what he had to say He
talked about the things that were and what
was still to be Now I don't know what the
future will bring but I hope that it will soon
begin It's said that the past repeats its self
well I am not one to scuff at fate But in this
case I hope that this is a wild mistake and
that this life we live today gets better each
and every day that's all I'll say*

By Donald Hoelscher

Just Sad

*Being sad is not so bad when you consider
all you had but there are times I'd have you
know that I wonder what makes you so there
is an answer of this I am sure but to find that
answer is a bore so I guess that all that can
be said is to crawl right back into your bed
and wish again for better times and get the
load off of your mind and if this sounds like
something you might try it sometimes works
I wouldn't lie some time as I wonder here
and there I see some people sit and stare and
wonder if they should go to bed and get the
bad thoughts out off their head*

By Donald Hoelscher

Just Saturday

Well the end the week is here at last and to lay in bed for as at long as it lasts but to some of us old people that don't last very long for we're used to being up by now and gone so we're trying to find something to do like a rummage sale or maybe a few there is not a thing that I really need but to visit with people is always fun and talk of places or things they have done well I guess since it's Saturday it's time to be on the go to meet new people and what they know and have to sell and so with these words I bid you ado and have some fun rummaging to

By Donald Hoelscher

Just wondering about

I as I sit here all alone I think back to a once happy home with a wife and family fair all gathered around the table there and cheer full talk about their days but like the time that's gone away and memories now is all I have to remember my lost happy past for like the things that are in the past I like them will go away I hope I will be remembered with a smile at least for a little wile

By Donald Hoelscher

Kids

As I sat listening the other day to some teenagers and what they had to say they talked of boys and the ones they liked but had not the nerve to say so out right at least to the boy's they had in mind so as they talked of what they would do I found it funny and so would you

By Donald Hoelscher

Kids and work

*In every morning there is the same mass
confusion and disarray of what to wear of
what to eat, of what shoes to put on their feet,
of watch the time, and wares my pills of we
have to hurry get to work I thought we were,
for once ahead and we should of gotten early
in to bed it seems that time just flies on by,
and we have got to go let's say goodbye and
out the door to start the day and hope that
nothing gets in our way as we hurry out and
on our way and it's off to work for the rest of
the day and than its home what more can you
say except to it's just a typical day*

By Donald Hoelscher

Kissing cousins

There was a girl I met in my long lost past and
we became friends but it didn't last for just to
be friends was not ok we wanted more that's
all I'll say and now as I look back on the past
I miss that love I thought would last for some
time later we both did wed to someone else
who now is dead so we did meet and tied the
knot were happy for a while but then were
not for things did happen as sometimes they
do and now were alone and I am not happy
I think of her both night and day and wish
she had not gone away but sometime she visits
and I must confess I treasure those times that
do not last and can't hardly wait for her
once more if I could have just one last wish
it would be to turn back the years to my long
lost past and have again that love I thought
would always last

By Donald Hoelscher

Lady Bus Driver

*She gets up early to start her bus so the kids
can have a nice warm bus but today's the day
just don't you know the bus decides it will
not go so as she fumes and frets and stumbles
around trying to figure what went down she
looks around and don't you know the cords
right there where it should go but not plugged
in so don't you know there is no where that
she can go so to the phone is her best bet and
call the boss and sit and fret about the pay
she will not get*

By Donald Hoelscher`

Last Good Bye

*I saw the angels calling me to leave this world
and forever be in the grave that's calling me
where there is no more pain or torture be
no more sickness down here on earth but I'll
miss my family and friends so with these last
words I'll let you know I'll pray for those still
down below but don't you worry or cry for
me I'll see you all by and by*

By Donald Hoelscher

Last Love

*Somewhere in my long lost past I thought I
had a love that would last but love like time
just slips away like the snow on the ground
on a sunny day and even when we say ok we
don't really know if it will last a day for love
like time is often fickle and leaves us in an
awful pickle of what to do and what to say to
make the pain just go away so if your heart
has been broken just hang on tight to what
was spoken of love that was of yesterday and
smile and say it will be ok because were made
of stronger stuff and the only way through it
is to suck it up*

By Donald Hoelscher

Another Night

Late last night as I lay in my bed thoughts of leaving passed through my head to a place where pain is no more and I journeyed along on that lonely shore I walked and I wondered aloud if this was the place the bible talked about or if this was some place where I would be lost and not see my Gods face as I stumbled about than with the dawning of days morning light I was still in my bed and not roaming about

By Donald Hoelscher

Last Night

*Last night in a dream filled night there was
someone there that seemed so right but to those
around said it will never work for she is not
the same you see and trouble is all you'll reap
but in my mind I said that I don't care and ill
do what my mind tells me that's hidden there
and take this girl to be my love and live my
life so just you all just leave us be*

By Donald Hoelscher

Last Night

*Last night as I lay in fitful sleep the dreams
I had kept me awake and made me think
of long lost days of old when my life was
something less so bold and I could do as I
liked and did not have to deal with quite so
much strife I wish there was a way to go on
today and forget about the bad things that
happened way back then and start my time
way back then*

By Donald Hoelscher

Late

*I snuck in the house the other night and tried
to be oh so quiet but don't you know my dear
old mom was up and roaming all around so
I got caught don't you know and when were
young we think were oh so slick and think we
know just every trick but there is one thing
that you should know moms may be old but
they ain't slow so if you're out for to deceive
don't mess with Mom you best believe*

By Donald Hoelscher

Library

Some time the kids take a trip to a place somewhere up town where all the people of long ago do seem to all abide there is animals of all sorts and outlaws friend and foe, spirits ghosts and goblins and history of old so when you're bored and need a break to the library you should go and enjoy the company of all the friends of people long ago so if you want there's movies, and music to 1 am told, cause it's been a wile myself and people say I am old.

By Donald Hoelscher

Lies and Innuendoes

*When you have a dream gone bad the pain
is still in your head and some time in your
heart as well and in places you will never tell
there is an answer of this I am sure but the
answer only confounds you more so in this
crazy mixed up world what to do is a furlong
guess and what to say is any one guess it seems
to some the answers clear but it's not there
heart that there to break and tear*

By Donald Hoelscher

Life's up and downs

When I think that life's real happy I get knocked down by something crappie like maybe someone in the dumps or may be gravy with lots of lumps or may be a car that's in my way that makes me to groan and say some well chosen words that don't sound great usually spiced with lots of hate, toward that person in that car or where he's at or his old car so if you think this poems the pits it's all because it's a bunch of spit.

By Donald Hoelscher

Life Is Fragile

In this time of toil and stress there comes a time of no more duress and as we look around we see people happy together still you see and living lives of love and peace and getting along with people that they meet

By Donald Hoelscher

Life of Men

*There is a time in and old man's life when
he hungers, for a wife someone to hold him
very tight and hold him through the long long
night a person he can call a friend who will
be with him until the end to be there when he
has to cry and when his friends pass him by
or life it seems has turned him down and be
there to help to rebound from all the cares of
yesterday and as this life draws to the end to
show him he still has a friend one that stands
by his side as long as he dose still abide and
when they lay him down to rest he will know
he still has had a friend who stood by him
until the end*

By Donald Hoelscher

Life with Arthur

*You get up each morning and its always the
same you don't need to look for you know
that its him once again for while you were
sleeping he's come around and he's bound
and determined to follow you around and
to make very sure there's not a muscle to be
found that don't hurt when you just move it
around it sounds kind a funny if you don't
know him now for when you get older he will
be always around so stock up on meds and
hope for the best and hope old author is going
to rest*

By Donald Hoelscher

Life's Problems

Each day we wake up with the hope of a good day and each day we face life's little things that make us wish we had never got up from our bed things like a car that won't start a tire that has gone flat or some one person that no matter how hard you try refuses to budge from his or her position even if you can show there wrong oh well I guess it would be right to say it's just another day

By Donald Hoelscher

Like A Parent

Like a parent here below our God looks after
us from above and guides us on our way if we
will but listen to what he says but like our
own children here with us we test his undying
love with things we do and say as we go on
our own chosen way and some time he must
feel betrayed from things we will do and say
but he has told us long ago that he loves us
and so he will forgive us for what we do and
say if we will return the love he has given to
each of us

By Donald Hoelscher

Liquid Sunshine

*There is things I should do but don't you know
it's raining outside and don't you know it
seems like it will probably rain all day so
anything outside will just have to wait and
there is grass to cut trimming to do and that's
just a very small sample of the things I could
do but if I look around I bet I could find
something inside to occupy my poor feeble
mind oh well I'll just have to say no use to
complain ill just rest and tomorrow another
day*

By Donald Hoelscher

Long Week End

*I guess I'll stay at home today For I can't
think of no place to go and time just seems so
slow with no one around but me I know and
I have no one I'd like to see at least not at this
present time you see for I have taken a place
inside where I have a place to hide and think
about my sad old life with a wish that I still
had a wife but that's not the way it is today
so I guess I'll just go on my way*

By Donald Hoelscher

Looking Glass

Did you ever see yourself standing by a mirror and wonder who this person was and how he did appear I wonder if the one we see is truly who we see or just a reflection of who we would like to be I some time wonder in this life if I am really the one and only me and not just a reflection of someone else I see

By Donald Hoelscher

Looking Up

*They say that things are looking up but the
ceilings here is all I got there must be something
that I missed but I don't know I must confess
and when I look outside I see the same old
work there is for you and me so is this thing
that they see some kind of mystical magic cal
thing maybe a psychic is what you need to
be to see the things that they see well I am
not one I must confess so I keep on stumbling
along with all the rest*

By Donald Hoelscher

Lost And Found

*If a dream is what you need I found one I
do believe or so I would like to think, I am
quite sure she is not aware of what my feelings
really are and though I don't know now for
sure I find myself at her door I always make
some sad excuse but in my heart I wonder if
this is really true and if this is the way she
would really feel but I also know that she is
too young for this old sad and lonely one*

By Donald Hoelscher

Lost And Found

*If a dream is what you need I found one I
do believe or so I would like to think, I am
quite sure she is not aware of what my feelings
really are and though I don't know now for
sure I find myself at her door I always make
some sad excuse but in my heart I wonder if
this is really true and if this is the way she
would really feel but I also know that she is
too young for this old sad and lonely one*

By Donald Hoelscher

Lost Dreams

*Last night in my sleep I dreamed of my life
and things and of my life the way it is and the
way that it should be I really am not certain
and I defiantly don't know why, I guess it
is up to me to just go on and try so I guess I
will stumble on and take things as they come
because there really is no good place for me to
try to run and hide and sometime I wonder
why that I am still here then some time I
understand that my time down here in this
world is all a part of the Master's plain   Still
Lost*

By Donald Hoelscher

Lost Fathers

*I joined the men of this great land to serve
my country was my great plan to protect my
friends and family here, in this great land
and so to travel to faraway lands, to fight for
freedom in there misguided lands and so you
see that I still am still right here where I fell
so tell, my friends and family, that I gave my
fair share, of blood and courage while over
here and tell my wife and children there at
home that there dad is watching from way
up here*

By Donald Hoelscher

Lost Time

As I sit here in this place, my mind does
wonder through time and space of days and
times of long ago, and people that I miss so. of
things that were said and wounds that bleed
and of people that are now long dead of times
I thought that I was wrong and times that I
was o so right arguments long in the night
and partners in my showed past what can I
say only that there is still always just another
day

By Donald Hoelscher

Love

Once I had a sweet little lady that drove me crazy some time maybe but love that girl I really did and then one day she went away and I don't mean by her choice I would have to say for the lord our God above took from me my one and only real true love

By Donald Hoelscher

Man

What is it that makes a man is it his size or may be the way he stands Is it something he does or the way that he stands or may be the things that he does The answer is said to be in the stars but me I am not and oracle or a witch so I don't really know So ill just pretend that I am wise and ill do the best that I know and always wonder why things turn out the way that they do

By Donald Hoelscher

Man Confused

*(Woman) in the garden of Eden the Lord
said man I'll give you a companion to hold
your hand and be with you and a partner
be and that's what happened to men you see
for not only do they hold your hand but also
your heart as well but if you think that this
ain't so close your eyes and you will know that
your life is wound around this theme and a
woman you know can be real mean and take
your heart in there schemes and then you will
be once more in the world alone and wonder
where to begin again to build your life with
another female friend*

By Donald Hoelscher

Marriage Partner

Some time in our life we look for a companion and a wife someone to be with us as we grow old and give us purpose and a goal and as our live does progress we tend to begin to regress and we need someone to push us along and help us again to be strong and to be alone is not the way to live our lives and that's all I'll say

By Donald Hoelscher

May Not Today

In our mind there is such a muddle and causes us so much trouble And makes us do things that we shouldn't and say things that we normally wouldn't oh well so much for the things of life and all this old crazy strife I see people everywhere that act like they really care but if the truth would be known it's all a show don't you know For I see people that put on a show and act like they really know But if they would be honest and tell it right they would not be able to sleep at night.

By Donald Hoelscher

Maybe

Christmas comes but once a year and people run around in doubt and fear of what to do or what to buy to please that woman man girl or boy I wonder what they would do if Christmas came every day or what they would do or what they would say to have a Christmas every day but to some of them that seems the case for everything they want or say just seems to come along their way

By Donald Hoelscher

McDonalds

*It's time for lunch the kids are alright and to
go to McDonald's to them is just right there
are big Mac fish and chicken and things ice
cream soda and sweet teas the thing the kids
are excited and to them threes no end the
play yards empty so where to begin there so
much excitement and it's such a great chore
to get them to eat at least some before you
turn them loose to the play yard again*

By Donald Hoelscher

Me

As I sat here this morning feeling all alone I ask the good Lord above to send me his love and also his help me to find someone to share this life and not be alone and with hope I must travel this journey of life searching again for a faithful wife someone like me that too is all alone and wants a companion and a happy home so with hope I'll start out again to find another lifelong friend and companion for life to be for me the love of my life

By Donald Hoelscher

Memories

As I sit here all alone I think back of a happy home where there was laughter everywhere and a wife and kids for me to share but life to us is not all fair and things we love soon disappear to be replaced with lots of memories of here and there and of the past for us to share so I guess what I am tiring to say is hold on tight to yesterday

By Donald Hoelscher

Mind Blank

I got up this morning my mind was a blank it was so foggy I couldn't even think so instead of a poem I turned on the TV just to see what the weather would be and its rain again don't you know and I sure have places that should really be and for sure some people to see and wouldn't you know that don't include sales that are a temptation to me all along my merry old way so you can see how busy will be checking on things I don't really need

By Donald Hoelscher

Missouri

*In old Missouri you never know one day rain
the next day snow one time it's warm the
next day cold but if really need to know go
to KRCG and so there is person that always
has an educated guess and so we listen with a
open ear just to see the lady appear to fill us
with words of wit and hope she's right and
not full of well you can guess all the rest*

By Donald Hoelscher

MOM

There is someone that's always there to help us with our hopes and cares but some time we don't think they understand but they can talk to us from first hand and remember that they too were young and probably done the things you've done so try not to be so hard on them for one time in the long lost past they too were young and had to ask OH MOM

By Donald Hoelscher

Mom

There is a person in our life that's always there with good advice Like brush your teeth, put on clean shorts, fold your clothes and do what's right Then one day as we grow up Mom becomes old and all wore out But there's one thing that never changes . . . she's still our Mom So as we lay her down to rest remember she has met the test and though she's gone she will still remain forever in our hearts Mom we'll miss you

By Donald Hoelscher

Mom and Dad

There are times when I feel like I am in jail
and there is no one near to go my bail and
the warden and the guards are always there
to keep me from the one that cares but to say
that I am abused would be just a big excuse
cause I am not allowed to run around all over
town with someone that they hardly know
so if we sit and think it out they have it all
figured out to save us from a big mistake to
us to a warden make

By Donald Hoelscher

207

More Hot Temperature

*This morning I got up turned the TV on to
hear some good news from the weather lady
that the hot weather was gone but wouldn't
you just know it there is no such luck the hot
stuff is on us and brother don't you know it's
hard to find a shady spot no matter where you
go so there is but one solution to this old hot
problem now so keep yourself inside the house
and outside never go*

By Donald Hoelscher

Mothers Day

There is a person in our life that stands by us through all our life and is always there through thick and thin and always ready to take us in and wipe our eyes when we cry but when her time down here is done well lose the most important one our Mother our MOM

By Donald Hoelscher

Mr. President

I agree with what you say and there should be another way to spend the taxes that we pay and make these troubles go away but when those in power can do just what they want without the voice of the peoples say than there has to be another way it seems like when you have milk in the fridge to long it becomes way to strong to drink or even use so to solve the problem you throw it out and start again that's what it's all about I believe that we have a lot of sour milk in Washington and it's time to throw them out and start again with new ideas

By Donald Hoelscher

My Aching Back

*When you get up and your one big pain and I
don't mean the one in the butt that you have
what is the best thing to do at this time but
moan and groan about better times when you
weren't bothered with the pain that you have
and transferred the source to some other kind
like the kids that you have or a love that has
gone bad or someone that is in your way and
the only choice that you have is sit there and
wait*

By Donald Hoelscher

My Body

*This is my body the one that when I look in
the mirror I see but let's really look and see
what you see is this person ok or do you wish
he would just go away some time I wish that
some would say I like you the way that you
are so don't go away but even as I think it I
know there's no way because sooner or later
I will go away*

By Donald Hoelscher

My Dad

There is a fellow we all know who worked real hard for us to know the simple things in this life he sent us on off to school where he hoped we would learn the golden rule like how to read and how to write and how to treat each other right but there is a time when he gets old and begins to forget what he's been told and wonders on like he don't care and some time when he's alone he ponders on his life and what went wrong and tries to live for the best and in his mind he has met the test

By Donald Hoelscher

My Dreams

In my dreams at night I long to hold someone tight and keep them always near and dry away each and every tear and hold them all through the night and tell them that every things alright for to be alone is not the way for some don't deal well with all alone that way and people need someone to talk with in the night and tell us that were alright there was a time when I believed that to be alone was just the way but every day becomes the same and loneness is such a pain

By Donald Hoelscher

My Friend

Thank you for the way you treat this old man when I visit there and thank you for the time you spent with me just yesterday, I have grown to look forward to my visits there it reminds me that to be alone is defiantly not the way her children are very courteous and respectful all the way she is a good friend and that's all there is to say

By Donald Hoelscher

My Kids

*Today I sat and turned back the time and
remembered my kids and about their time
and how they were when they were young
and who they are now that they're gone it's
funny how you can see mistakes and foolish
things they do and take and even if you say
it's dumb it's up to them right or wrong so
being old is not so good for it hurts to see them
in their strife and the mistake's they make in
their life and you know that what you do are
say will only drive them farther away*

By Donald Hoelscher

My Life

*How many times have you heard someone say
life is fine and going my way then like a bad
dream we wake up and find that everything
it seems has turned all around and bad luck
has settled on our home town and we say to
our self this can't happen to me and I this is
a lesson and you best believe that good things
happen to bad people and bad things happen
to good people*

By Donald Hoelscher

My Long Days

There was a time when life was fine and I was busy all the time with work and family and kids of mine and working hours of overtime and people around with things to do and party's for kids and even school with foot ball games and plays and things and even band concurs there at school but now all of that's all in the past and I wonder how long this boredom will last for when your old the things back then won't be even thought again

By Donald Hoelscher

My Mind

*Last night I took a walk into the recesses of
my mine just to see just what I would find
and while I was there I saw things of my long
lost past and wondered as a strolled why they
didn't last and all I could figure out was that
my mind on some things was a blank on a lot
of things in my long lost past*

By Donald Hoelscher

My Thoughts

Today as I lay in bed different thoughts went through my head and as I lay I wondered why these things had come to me and if it was something that was to be I have heard since I was young that good things are to come well I am still waiting this I know so if this is something that's meant to be I hope it's soon that's all I'll say

By Donald Hoelscher

My Thought

If we could change this life we lead I wonder what we could do to make this world safe for me and you and get people to stop and think about what they do and what they say and make this pain and misery go away and be a friend to those around and spread this feeling to all around it seems like once a year these feelings do appear and we wish to those all around good will to all at least for a day or so

By Donald Hoelscher

My Time

As I sit here in this place my mind drifts through time and space to the time of yesteryear when life was less hectic and so I fear that before this life is through there is bound to be some good times too I some time wish there was a way to turn the time back to another day and live again the good times there but alas there is no way to go back to that time away back then and live the past we had again

By Donald Hoelscher

New Life

I get up each morning to greet the new day with a sense of purpose and the thought of a great day but then the feeling of loss seems to lead me astray to the feeling of alone and dread of one more day but to carry on is the thing I must do for somewhere out there is a me and you and the hope of tomorrow and the years of the future with someone new that will be with me always to live together until this life is through

By Donald Hoelscher

Night

The sun goes down the stars come out and eyes get heavy as you curl up tight and as you snuggle in for a long long night then dreams come marching on in your sleep and reminds you of things that could not be and you toss and turn in your sleep and hope that at least something bad won't happen to you and me so as the day slips away I guess that all I can say is when the night time comes just go to bed and hope for pleasant dreams instead

By Donald Hoelscher

Night

Some time you feel like the nights to long and you feel like you're all alone and dreams of things of yesterday just seem to have their own way and the time just seems to stop and you know that time is all you got what do you do to ease your mind and try to pass this long old time some time you wish that you could see the end and so you try to pretend that this is a better day and try to forget your sad nights of yesterday

By Donald Hoelscher

No Love

*Be careful my friends when you fall in love
for they may look like they came from the
heavens above but look real hard and you
might see that what they bring is not good
for you are me so if a dream is what you see
I wish you luck for this is not always what is
to be and a broken heart is what you'll have
and loneliness is what you'll reap*

By Donald Hoelscher

No Money

There are some folks in this life that to them the world seems quite so fine but they don't fight from day to day just to earn their piddling pay and to them the world seems quite ok and even if there way is not quite ok and if you are not one of those chosen few this state of the world is the spits to you and if you think I missed spelled a word just don't be quite so absorbed for I am quite aware of the word I used and it's not a mistake I am telling you

By Donald Hoelscher

No More

*I woke up this morning got up off my bed trying
to find a way to hold my fool head looked for
some tooth picks for to keep my eyes open my
voice was so hoarse from screaming sit down
that I can't hardly speak oh well so much for
the good times and the long loss of sleep but
when I get home you better believe that this
old man is going to bed with no reprieve*

By Donald Hoelscher

No Place like Home

It's funny when you get older that when once you were so bold that this all changes as you get older I find that the things that once I thought were just a walk in the park seems like a trek up a mountain side and time spent away from our safe place seems like forever I don't have an answer to this all I know for sure is time away from home is and experience not looked forward to and a trip somewhere is locked to a trip back home why is this I wish I knew

By Donald Hoelscher

No Rest

*As a busy parent there's lots to do to get the
kids all ready for school than there's the thing
of going to work and finding time for home
work and if you're lucky and things work out
right you'll get to sleep some more to night
but like the times the previous night you're
so wound up and that isn't right so you'll lay
right down and toss and turn with thoughts
of where to begin again*

By Donald Hoelscher

No Rest for the Wicked

I woke up this morning and as I lay in bed
thoughts of staying there ran through my head
of what to do or what to say to make this
feeling just go away I see the things on the TV
about the weight systems and losing weight it
makes me wonder if that should I try these
gadgets and pay the price of prolonged agony
and moan and groan of pro longed pain and
crip around like I am older than I am oh
well I just told myself to get right up and stop
feeling all this stuff and feeling sorry just
doesn't help so I guess I'll just go on to work

By Donald Hoelscher

No Time

There is a time in all our lives when we get tired of the troubles of this old life and wish for something better or at least a change to somewhere else I wish there was a way to make these feelings of today go away but as of yet I haven't found the way to even get around the things of every day and the time here alone seems to be always there to sit alone and stare at things and also yet another day so if you're lucky and find a mate hang on tight make no mistake

By Donald Hoelscher

No Time

Some time in this world we get so tied up in this life that we fail to see the forest for the trees and it seems that no matter which way we go it's wrong those are the days when we want to just crawl in a hole and pull the covers in on us I guess the only other solution is to just say oh well tomorrow is another day

By Donald Hoelscher

No Time for Me

*I had a thought just today of this crazy world
and the things people do and say about the
world and my crazy life and how when your
alone you miss a wife I wish there was a way
to be free and also say my partner is the one
I love and to be with her still makes my life
so even if we are apart she knows she still has
my heart*

By Donald Hoelscher

No Way

I wish there was a way to save a very special day one day in our life which we could spend for the whole eternity but we don't have a simple choice and the life we have is not totally ours the Lord put us down here to sink or swim and change some simple things so as our life goes on we just do the best we can and hope to meet our God at the very end

By Donald Hoelscher

Not Crazy Yet

As I lay's in dreamless sleep I longed for
someone here to keep The feelings of a lone to
stay far from this old man's day To be alone
is a pain and to talk to one self is surely the
pits for you always know what the answer is
even before the question is ask They say to
have and intelligent conversation one must
talk to yourself And you know that crazy is
right on the border line to that and I don't
think I am crazy yet But some time I wonder
how close I really am

By Donald Hoelscher

Oh My

*I got home it was early in the morning and
the bed looked appealing but the time was not
there so I stretched out for a short period of
time trying to clear the cob webs from my mind
but the memories of last night kept running
through my mind and sleep was fleeting at
least for a while the little man that lives in
my head kept pounding to get out so I guess I
will sleep and put him out of my head*

By Donald Hoelscher

Old Man's Thoughts

*When you get older the things that we need
seems to be farther away don't you see and
even if were quite able to see our arms seem
to be shorter when we try to read are longer
as some times it may seem and to walk very
far is a pain in the neck are maybe even lower
than our back I believe so I guess that what I
am trying to say is don't get older go the other
way I know from experience and that's all for
now that I'll say*

By Donald Hoelscher

Old Night Time

*Each night as I lay in dream filled sleep I
think of someone soon to meet and make my
time down here so neat with a mate with me
to stay and never ever go away but a dream
is just a dream and no matter how we scheme
we will never ever make someone stay if they
want to go away it is said for each of us there
is a mate so take your time make no mistake
I heard one time that even a dog will find his
own bone*

By Donald Hoelscher

Old Santa Claus

Its once again that time of year when all of our hopes and dreams do appear and we again look forward to that jolly old man that brings us some things to make us happy again but there are some places that he doesn't go for people live in shanty's and there isn't no joy and the kids all know that today is the same and to them a good meal is all they can hope to receive so to all these people I say once again may the Lord bless you this year once again

By Donald Hoelscher

Old Thoughts

*In my dreams at night I see the world out
there according to me an sometime this world
just isn't right as you watch people in their
plights I wonder if the maker does see all that's
happening to all you see or if he chooses what
is to be and leaves them in their own misery
there's people left and right doing things that
are not right and think they own the world
they see and the heck with all the rest of you
and me*

By Donald Hoelscher

On A Limb

When it seems like you're out on a limb just drop your ladder and start again and as we begin to start anew we know the things are there are to do and try the life that we now have that had once seemed so bad and change the things that make it bad with smiles and happiness all around and drop those blues that get us down

By Donald Hoelscher

Once a Dream

There once was a people that had dreams of what their life would soon be and what they would see but dreams are often fickle and they often lost hope and life to them seemed like some old sick joke with constant crises both to left and to right and it seems to them like this life is all one big fight for what they needed and what they thought was right

By Donald Hoelscher

Once I was happy

There was a man that I once knew that had all the things he was entitled to but life did change as life would do and now he sits and ponders anew of what his life was coming to and where his life was going to some day and I wish I knew what the next day will be happy or blue sometime this old world just seems to be like a big old puzzle with a piece missing for me and you and we look around the whole day through for the last piece until this life is through

By Donald Hoelscher

Once In Every Life

Some time in this life we find the one we have looked for so many times in our life someone who just there smile makes us feel like we're on top of the world and looking down on everything that is happening to those around us and feeling sorry for those people who have yet to find that special someone to brighten there place in life whether it be a husband wife or just a close friend

By Donald Hoelscher

Once Upon A Time

Once upon a time there was a man that
thought he found a friend someone he could
talk to when he was alone again and feeling
down and out but it didn't take too long
to finally find things out that the friend he
thought he had was always nowhere about so
to finally solve the problem and to live this
feeling out he done other things to keep his
life on track and vowed to forget the one who
had done the turn about

By Donald Hoelscher

Only This Morning

As I lay and tried to sleep thoughts of leaving
came to me
and reminded me again that some time in
my future there would be a pain I would have
to bear and I would have no one else to share
For travel to that heavenly home is only for
us alone so I guess what I am trying to say is
live your life the safest way and listen to your
conscience and be on guard for some time
soon you may be called

By Donald Hoelscher

Orion Science Center

There is a place in old Camdenton town where lots of fun can be found you can launch a rocket up in space, explore in a pit or ride a liftosaurus up real quick then launch a water balloon at a dinosaur then zip down a pterodactyl glide explore the long old solar tubes or launch the old trebuchet or if you're brave take a swing through a swampy glade or if a remembrance you desire there are things for kids and even you and remember it don't cost a mint to have a remembrance what do you think

By Donald Hoelscher

Our Life

In this life we live down here is filled with sorrow doubts and fears of what might happen to make us all our feelings hide and try to fool each other's eyes by trying to show there's nothing wrong to hide he is the one who always knows the one whose love will always be there to answer all our needs and cares for he has told us long ago how much he loves us all so and if we will but choose to believe he will answer all our needs

By Donald Hoelscher

Out side

I awoke this morning and looked outside the snow was falling from the sky the trees were covered with a blanket of white and the snow was shining in the dawns early light no artist at his very best can compete there is no contest for our god above is the master of all with the beauty of winter or the beauty of fall and then we have the flowers in spring and the birds and bees as there ritual begins

By Donald Hoelscher

Past Time

Can you imagine just yesterday we were so young and on our merry way with only a few problems and such and now they all come to us in a terrible rush I wish there was a way to save yesterday but to my small brain there just isn't no way some time I can remember some things from the past but they don't last long so don't even ask but I can remember my love from the past and it still hurts so don't even ask

By Donald Hoelscher

Politics

When were in school we were taught the golden rule of reading writing and arithmetic but little did we know that reading some of these documents that are put before us are anything but lots of double talk that tend to beat around the preverbal bush so bad that we can get absolutely and totally confused by their Bull Spit so to understand the reasoning behind there double talk you would have to make them explain in simple words which is in some cases not possible for there so out on a limb that they them self's don't understand

By Donald Hoelscher

Questions

*Do you ever feel like you have the answer
before the questions ask? Or have you ever
gone somewhere and know what was there, or
talk to someone and know what they're going
to say or feel like the time is slowly slipping
away. it's said that getting older is what there
is to blame, but I am not so sure of that at
least in my mind so I'll just have to live with
this at least for today, or what else is there
to do to make it go away now if you know
the answer I wish you tell me true for than
I wouldn't have to wonder till my days are
through*

By Donald Hoelscher

Rain and Lighting

*Outside the clouds are moving fast it hard
to tell how long the calm will last are when
the rain will start falling down to soak the
earth with one more round there are those
who will complain about the constant falling
rain but me I know this for sure you best stay
inside your doors especially when the lighting
slowly runs around I can remember when I
was young the rain to me was so much fun*

By Donald Hoelscher

Rainy Day

*I woke up this morning and looked outside
the rain was a falling down from the sky
It looked like the clouds had become like
a sponge and the angels were having just so
much fun a splashing and sending the water
on down and soaking everything down on the
ground in the course of their fun so I guess
the thing for us for us all to do is carry and
umbrella or a jacket might do*

By Donald Hoelscher

Relationships

*There is a time when the truth is not there
and no matter how hard you try to stay cool
they keep on taking and breaking each simple
rule the rules of a relationship are simple
to some but an effort to others if you are
the one who is always there when there is
something to do to lend a helping hand and
help them get through then there are those
that think they can do whatever they wish
and it's alright with you so if this is true and
you are the one who thinks it's alright to walk
on someone a lie still hurts that's all that ill
say remember your time will come and you'll
remember someday the friend that you try to
keep pushing away*

By Donald Hoelscher

Sad but True

*I this crazy life we live we try hard to forgive
and yet we find our self's in a place where we
don't belong I some time wonder if its fate
or if we do this to ourselves there are times I
sure wish I knew but then I am like me or you
we do things and make these plans that seem
to get so out of hand we hope and pray that
it will work but some time we feel just like a
jerk for life is not always what it seems and
this is true you best believe*

By Donald Hoelscher

Sad Story

*I had a friend I like you to know we were
close I want you to know and if there was
something that I would need he was always
there for me and as the years went slowly by
we both got old I don't know why but I guess
it was just a fact of life and now he's gone and
I still wonder why but it isn't up to us to say
when the lord will call us all away so that's
the way it goose God called him away so to
heaven he sure went*

By Donald Hoelscher

Sandy Ground

Don't build your life on sandy ground for it will only let you down and shift away like the sands of time and leave you all alone and crying and make you seek some brand new place that you can again call your space this place be sure to anchor tight to someone dear to hold you tight and be right there through thick and thin and never leave you alone again this is to some a hopeless dream and no matter how hard they wish the truth is not there this I believe

By Donald Hoelscher

School Days

I drove past the church in the sunshine so
clear and out of the school the kids did appear
and head for the church to wait for the priest
to begin with the mass then back to the school
and school to begin the teachers were there
in the class rooms doing their best to get the
students to start with their test for the end of
school was soon to arrive said the teachers to
each other with a long sigh

By Donald Hoelscher

Schools End

*It was may twenty second the end of the year
the kids were ecstatic and ready to cheer the
teachers were trying to hold it all in for they
like the kids couldn't wait for the summer
to begin and time to do nothing unless they
so chose but not quite so for mothers of those
kids there at home so once more again the
child care begins to set in and they will look
forward for the summer to end and school
to begin*

By Donald Hoelscher

Schools First Day

*Its early morning and the kids aren't awake
and we just woke up and there must be some
mistake because this just can't be the first day
of school and as the kids wake up confusion
the rule so as we try to sort out the fog in our
minds we try to get everyone ready and its
almost time for that big yellow limousine to
arrive and pick up our kids and we relax with
a sigh and hope that things will get better at
least by tomorrow*

By Donald Hoelscher

Schools End

*When we are born our journey begins and
we set out not knowing for sure the location
where the journey will end so as we sail on in
the boat we call life sometime we're lucky and
find a good wife so then like before were tossed
on the waves and find ourselves wondering if
we've found the right place where we at long
last can drop our anchor and forget the long
voyage and the place we began for we have
been told we will leave this ship some day and
fly to the heavens with God as our Captain
and the Angels the crew*

By Donald Hoelscher

Shadow Lady

There is a woman that haunts my dreams at night and leaves me a wishing I could hold her tight and it makes me wonder if my long lost past has come to haunt my dreams at last and if this is to be my fate than that's ok I can relate for that love was the first one true love that made me feel like I belonged to someone true without a doubt and though she's gone the flames not out

By Donald Hoelscher

Sick

*Not tonight I have a head ache that's what
you tell yourself when everything you try
to do seems like and extreme effort and the
thought of doing anything seems to be an
impossibility oh well I'm sick and the little
critter in my belly is bound and determined
to see that food will not stay in there for any
amount of time what so ever so I guess I will
just lay there and die and that can't be so for
to die I would have to get better oh well that
can't be a bad idea so get better*

By Donald Hoelscher

Slippery When Wet

*Outside the clouds are covering our pretty
sunshine and the water is just continually
pouring down and the drive way looks like
a big old stream and there are things to do
don't you believe and I am so   disappointed
I am just about to go insane cause the things
I really need do I just have to put off once
again oh well so I guess I must confess it gives
me time for this old body to rest*

By Donald Hoelscher

Snow

I look outside to see if what they said has come to be and sure as the world the snow did come and the ground is white and the snow is still falling down the lord has sent his blanket of white to cover the world with his pure blanket of white and the moans and groans of the people down here has already begun for the Christmas season will soon to be here and the people down here will be scurrying around looking for the perfect gift for those around parents will be an absolute mess figuring out which toy is best
By Donald Hoelscher

Soggy Rainy Day

I looked outside and don't you know the rain was a falling down from the sky the frogs were looking for the high ground and the cat fish were crawling up on to the banks looking for some shallow water to rest well I guess you know that this is not true and you know that I am just fooling with you oh well I guess we can always run between the drops that is if your skinny enough well all I can say is that is defiantly not me for the space between the drops would have to be as wide as a big oak tree for me to get missed just fun you see

By Donald Hoelscher

Some Say

*Some say Christmas is a time for joy but not
for this old lonely boy for to be alone this time
of year is not a time for all this cheer for some
time when we are alone we find our self's in
a sad old gloom that drags us down to a place
we defiantly would rather not want to be and
so as we try to make things better we'll try to
get along better with another*

By Donald Hoelscher

Some Time

*There are times in our way ward quest when
we need to take a kind a rest and take stock of
what we have and forget about our crazy past
then with luck we can begin again to sort out
our life and start again there isn't any simple
way to say the things we need to say except
to say oh well we will try again it's just once
more another day*

By Donald Hoelscher

Sometime

Some time in my dreams at night I hold you
oh so tight but then in the morning light I
realize that one that I held so tight was just
a dream and I know I just had just another
wishful scheme and if a dream is all I have it
can't be just all that bad for if my dreams is
all I have I guess it can't be all that bad

By Donald Hoelscher

Sometime I think

There are times I think our life's a book and no matter where we look there is no way for us to know just where our life is bound to go for all the plans that we strive to make it seems like there is a turn life is bound to take and leave us out there high and dry and wondering just why so we don't remember where we begin but we do know where we will end

By Donald Hoelscher

Song

There was a time in my very long lost past when I found me a girl and a love I thought would last but some time these things are not true and they come back home to you They leave you all alone and no place to call your home So my advice to you is to find someone that you know is true and don't leave her all alone and you won't be blue and you can keep you wife and happy home

By Donald Hoelscher

Sons and Daughters

*When you have kids you think when they
grow up that you're free to run all again all
about but then the reality begins to set in and
you begin to realize that being a parent does
never end for its mom I need this and dad I
need that and can you take care of the kid s
while we go out and then when you think that
life is beginning to end the grand kids move
in and we start all over again with grand
maw do this and grand paw do that so ass
this poem ends just like it bargain just being
a parent just never ends*

By Donald Hoelscher

Spark of Life

*Somewhere from up there in time and space
there comes a life for each of us And it isn't
something that we can plan for it is only in
our God's hands For he sees us all from up
above and shares with us his undying love He
sends his angels from heaven's door to guide
us in our earthly chores And all he asks from
each of us is to love what he has sent us for
And remember that our lives are not for us
alone but to do his will and for him alone,*

By Donald Hoelscher

Spell Christmas

*This is the time that comes once a year a time
for all people to be of good cheer and treat
each other as they should every day and it's
sad but true that really don't happen but
wouldn't it be nice if this could be so and we
could always know which way to go but to
bad for us this life is not clear and we just
wonder around for another whole year as I
sit here this morning and think of the past I
wonder how long I will last*

By Donald Hoelscher

Strange

It's strange how when you visit relatives and friends in hospitals and things how your mind wonders to life's bitter end and dwells on the things of the life that will end where we'll join all our long lost friends I some time wonder when I leave this old world if I'll be missed by those here below or if like time the memories of me will just slip away and they will all live just for today

By Donald Hoelscher

Summer Break

How is it that when you get the time your
broke and don't have a dime to do the things
you looked forward too for a long time and it
seems like the days just seem to fly and before
you know it the time is here to begin to do
what you do all year oh well when you have no
choice you go do the job and stifle your voice
for you know that it's the time once more to
go to work and don't worry any more

By Donald Hoelscher

Sure Would Be Nice

*It sure would be nice to say that everything
is going my way and to some that just might
be ok but to some of us I have to say that this
world has sure gone to spit and the longer
were in it the more crappie it gets oh well so
much of this is sure the pits and I don't know
just what to think of it so ill bide my time and
hope and pray for at least a semblance of a
better day*

By Donald Hoelscher

Table of Excuses

The best to the worst I am tired I worked all night I don't know where the time went I over slept and My car won't start The kids were sick and I was up most of the night My alarm didn't go off or I didn't hear it The best is dam I really didn't want to go to work or church any way I didn't really want to go in to work I have a head ache All the old man wanted to do was fuss all night so I got no sleep

By Donald Hoelscher

Thanksgiving

This is the day to be happy and gay to greet others we pass on our way and treat others like we really care and greet those around us and be willing to smile and share some time I think that there is nothing to be thankful about when someone you once loved has turned you about and you feel like you should be happy and shout but all those feelings are now all shut up inside like some big old vault well I guess I should be happy and not be so sad and think of the good times that I once had
By Donald Hoelscher

The Ache

*There are some pains that you can't see and
those are them that bother me like a woman
that treats you oh so cold and makes your
heart feel oh so old then there are those that
just plain hurt like a back that has gone plain
berserk are maybe your legs that feel so weak
some time and you wonder why you feel like
you could cry but it's said that a man is not
suppose to cry so you just sit there in your
misery and wonder how to begin again*

By Donald Hoelscher

The Black Hole

Did you ever have a time in your life when
everything in your life seemed to be going in
a downhill spiral that there is no way to get
out of and even in your dreams you fight to
get your mind in a state that you can function
in your everyday life it's said that after fifty
you enter the golden age my thoughts are bull
if its golden I have yet to find my gold

By Donald Hoelscher

The Book

Once I thought that life was a single book
of one story but I have since learned that in
fact the life we lead is a serious of stories with
each one a different episode of the same life
so that we have trouble trying to figure out
one ending from the next beginning so the life
we live is and ongoing story of confusion and
heart ache joy and confusion

By Donald Hoelscher

The Call

The phone did ring this very day and as I listened to what they had to say memories of the past did come to me and the things I did than I could see there are times I wish I could change the things of my past and make this life the good things last but time is a cruel task master and we either learn or get left by the way so with this thought I close this poem and leave the thought back in the past where it belongs

By Donald Hoelscher

The Child

There once was a little girl who
cried most every day then one day she stopped
her tears were gone and they took the little
girl away to a place were tears were no more
and smiles were on the way for she was with
the lord above what more is there to say

By Donald Hoelscher

The Church

*The church is just what it is just a building
be a place to gather people to worship the
deity our God above I believe a church is
just a building and our God is in you and
me and when we go to church we take him
into the building there with you and me and
as we get down on our knees we ask him for
our needs and he will answer in his way and
help us in our grief and show us the way our
life should really be for he is there to help us
and show us his way our life is now and will
surely be but we will have to listen and not
just with ears but also with our heart's for it
will always hear the voice of our creator who
made you and me*

By Donald Hoelscher

The Creek

When we were young and down on the farm
there was a creek that ran right through our
farm and when it would rain we head for the
garage to find those inner tubes we had laying
around then head for the creek farther on up
so we could ride the tube on the waves it would
buck but watch for the fence and don't get
tangled around for you would be in trouble
and probably drown but we were luckily and
the fun did abound and the memories of fun
in the past still come around

By Donald Hoelscher

The Day

*Did you ever have a day when everything
just came your way and you find yourself in
and awful pickle for what you said and that
means trouble for you find you have to do
some things that you didn't really mean but
commit your self is what you did so you do the
deed you really didn't mean oh well I guess
this is the way of life and its always full of
strife there is a saying I once heard about
opening mouth and inserting foot*

By Donald Hoelscher

The Dike

There once was a little boy who lived very far away In a place called Holland or so the book does say he was a very curious little boy and one day as he passed the dam he saw that there was a leak so he put his finger into the hole to steam the stream of water but as he stood there all alone there was no one he could call to help him with his plight at all I now know the felling for I had my share of water as I set out to fix a leak the water went ever ware and there was no one that I could call to help so by the time the leak was fixed I was soaking wet and the morel of this story is to always have some help
By Donald Hoelscher

The Dinner

There is this lady that I know we have become good friends and so she did invite me to her house to eat and to me that sounded really sweet the dinner was so very good and I enjoyed it that's understood I find myself thinking about her often through the day and if I was somewhat younger I be chasing her every day but an old man like me is not what she needs she has four kids and I believe that's more than enough responsibly I believe

By Donald Hoelscher

The Donation

*I went to church last Sunday with a little
girl of five and waited for collection time to
finally arrive she kept on asking me when
the time would be, for the collection basket
to come to her and me, I had given her some
change to put there in the basket but she had
her own idea and I wander what they will
say when they count the money or if they will
throw the gift away for she had given what
she had and I am proud to say that she had
given   everything she had at least this one
Sunday   Just Chloe*

By Donald Hoelscher

The Dream Lady

*I had a dream the other night about someone
to hold me tight and stay with me for a while
to be near this old man and make me smile
someone to talk to in the night to be there to
hold me tight and tell me that I'll be alright
a good friend is what I need to patch me up
when I bleed not just the kind that makes a
mess some time from my eyes I must confess
for this lonely ness is driving me to the brink
of insanity though I try to keep real busy the
feelings keep on haunting me   Alone!!!!*

By Donald Hoelscher

The Fairy Tales

When I grew up stories were all the rage and
we couldn't wait to read the next page but life
for us is not the same today and there is not
just another page but still I wonder which is
real the things that I read or the way I feel I
read the paper and see the news and wonder
if it's really real or if this is just another story
too

By Donald Hoelscher

The Fantasy Story

There once was a couple that had a sweet dream that to be together was the real thing but they never planed on the joker called fate who could wreck all their plans and leave them in a terrible state so that you don't know where to go to get yourself fixed and wonder around like you have made a mistake to others around the solution is clear just get on your horse and ride out of there but some of us don't have any stable so we still walk around with our chin on our chest and try to do our very best
By Donald Hoelscher

The Flake

I wonder what it would be like to just drift
on down in silent flight and after the trip to
earth was done just lay around on the ground
and wait for the sun to once more shine to
take me back up to the heavens just one more
time and as I wonder about all of this all id
wait again for the time to fall and again to
enjoy the trip just one more time and not
worry where the trip would end

By Donald Hoelscher

The Fool

Last night in a crazy dream I had my love
right next to me and it was grand for a little
while for I woke up this morning with a silly
smile so don't tell me that dreams don't help
for some time they feel so real and so I will live
in dreams again until the one I love becomes
so real that in my arms I can really feel the
love that I still hunger for

By Donald Hoelscher

The Fourth

*I often ask myself what this day is all about
and the answer is always the same the birth
day of our freedoms gained so to celebrate this
day I guess I'd just have to say the noise that is
all around seem to me so quite profound and
all that I can say is thank our god for in his
way he has given us all a better way*

By Donald Hoelscher

The Globe

*Have you ever wondered if when you shake a
snow globe you see the rain and see the snow
with things surrounding us here down below
the thought has occurred that all of this is so
I some time wonder but I really don't know
and for now and the rest of this life I'll just
have to go on wondering and put up with
thoughts of not knowing what this is all about
but still wish I knew*

By Donald Hoelscher

The Good Bye

*As the time draws near for her to leave I find
myself saying please don't go for I need you
so but still I know someone needs you to and
in your mind your doing the best you can do
I wish there was a way to change the time
to back when you were mine but time don't
move back in that way so in the now I'll have
to stay but still I wish that there was a way to
keep you here or make you stay*

By Donald Hoelscher

The Guide

What is it that tells us not to go astray and guides us on our way to that place up there above where all our loved ones up there do dwell and as we wait with patient hope that someday we to can from this world elope to be again with the ones who have gone before to be with god on that golden shore

By Donald Hoelscher

The Hog Fiasco

*Did you ever have a night when everything
went wrong and you think that why is this
happing to me and how could this thing come
to be what I am talking about is hauling a hog
to the fair early last night and just to get the
trailer ready was such a fight but we loaded
the hogs and made it to the fair but then the
trouble really began when we when we ready
to leave the fair the hog was not ready to go
and told us so don't you know with squealing
and snorting and jumping around we finally
got him loaded and started for home and he
jumped from the trailer and started roaming
around we roped him down and loaded him
again and were soon home ward bound and
home again*

By Donald Hoelscher

The House

*Many years ago when I was gone a letter come
to me and I was informed that my parents
had bought them a small mine farm the land
was five acres and you had to cross a creek
and the house was small and not modern you
see and if the urge hit you in the middle of the
night the path was long and it didn't seem
right and when it was cold the sidewalks were
tin and you had to be careful when you tried
to get in are you would find yourself looking
up at the stars from a awkward position flat
on your back but it was home for a little while
so as I think about it I can't help but smile*

By Donald Hoelscher

The Kid

*Life is fragile handle with love as I looked
in the eyes of a little girl I saw the feelings of
this crazy world that dwelled right there on
her face and heard the words of this troubled
place and I to felt the same on that day and
saw this life as some weird game of silly words
and crazy dreams like the life of this little girl
it leaves you feeling sad also in this weird and
crazy mixed up world*

By Donald Hoelscher

The Ladder

I knew a man one time that struggled to climb to the top of the ladder and as he tried something happened to the man and he forgot what he was after so as he wondered around this crazy world he never found the peace that he was after so I guess its save to say as you struggle for the top some time it's a whole lot better to be satisfied with what you got

By Donald Hoelscher

The Lady

There once was a lady that I know who was
special id like you to know but it seems like
the years took that away and made me think
a different way so if there is someone that you
think is great think real hard and not make
a mistake for life can be so cruel to you and
leave you all alone and blue just remember
love is a fickle thing and can leave you back
were you began

By Donald Hoelscher

The Law

*What was formed so long ago was to protect
us all this I know and it wasn't to prosecute
the innocent this I believe but to help to find
the answer sure so why do we see these things
that leave us all to believe the worst of people
here and not a chance for us to hear the truth
of what happened and then to believe and
not to convict someone and innocent friend*

By Donald Hoelscher

The Lie

There was a man one time that thought that
what was said was right at the time some
time just what we hear is not the thing for us
to revere but blind faith is all we have so it
makes it hard to forgive when un truth is told
and they say it all so bold and you wonder
just what to believe every time that they speak
for every lie just seems to grow every time
that it's told

By Donald Hoelscher

The Life umbrella

*Last night while I sleep I saw something that
made me wake and that was a simple thing
that people use now and then to protect them
self's from sun and rain and then I thought
wouldn't it be nice to use the same to protect us
from all that harms like the pain of loneness
or the fear of things that make us weep or
deprive us from rest full sleep*

By Donald Hoelscher

The Long Breath

In the beginning of this life When we a born
we fight for life and in the end the results
the same we fight for one more breath again
and if we're lucky we catch that air and live
again in this hemisphere and the mystery of
this world is this when it's our time we cease
to exist and the soul that is our self moves on
to a better place where we came from

By Donald Hoelscher

The long Day

*To get up early that's ok but it sure makes for
a very long day and it seems like the time just
seems to drag, and as the day draws to an end
we hurry on our way back home again, where
we have been for an hour or so and you just
bet were ready to go we get into our car or
truck and prepare our self's for the traffic to
buck and we try our best to meet the test and
keep our tempers there in check and smile
at those who are in our way and as for now
that's all I'll say*

By Donald Hoelscher

The Lord Called

*The Lord has called Dolores from up above to
share with him his everlasting, and promised
love and to the ones that's left behind he tells
us that we too will join them again on our
chosen time and as we linger on down here
we will wait for him again to appear to tell
us that our time is come to join again our
lost loved ones so as we say our last good by
remember we too will join them by and by*

By Donald Hoelscher

The Miracle

*In a land far away a child was born on
Christmas day one to save us all from sin and
bring us back home to heaven again it does
seem to me that on this day and time that we
have forgotten what happened on this day
and turned our minds on something else so
I believe it's time to go back once again and
remember that Christmas is here again and
why we celebrate this holy day*

By Donald Hoelscher

The Monkeys Are Loose

School is out hip hip hurray The teachers are free after today No more lesions for you to prepare You finally have time for the family to share Good bye Kids see you next year

By Donald Hoelscher

The Moon

*As I drove home just to night I had a thought
that all was right but still I wondered what
was to be and when we go does someone
welcome me are if I am to be alone and forever
on this earth to roam I have a feeling and I
hope it's so that there is someone awaiting so
I'll just go on and do my best and hope when
I go to rest that I won't be alone and God will
forgive me and bring me home*

By Donald Hoelscher

The Mystery

Today is a wait and see we never know when it will be or what can happen are if we'll see what is coming for you and me so to those of us who worry still and wonder if it's his will for us to live longer down here below are if soon it will be time for us to go but to those of us who sit and grieve I believe it because we don't believe that we to will someday go and leave this place and be with our God up there in space

By Donald Hoelscher

The New Priest

Each Sunday I head off to church to visit with our lord in his own house and as I sit and anticipate the mass and await the priest who is to celebrate the service I can't help but wonder what the sermons about and try to find peace wile people are wondering in and out I can't help but wonder as I hear the good news of God's word how I can use it for the next week or two so if you're like me sit up and listen and don't be sleeping or looking around sit up and listen while the word is put out

By Donald Hoelscher

The Old Fellow

*There is this old man that lives up the street
who always seems to be so sweet and never a
harsh word does he say no matter what the
time of day he always smiles and say's good
day no matter if its rain or shine and leaves
us with a happy smile that makes us wonder
what there is that keeps him always so upbeat
may be its something that we all need to keep
us too so all up beat*

By Donald Hoelscher

The One

*When you're young your parents say just wait
and some day the time will come and you will
find someone that is your match in every way
well that's ok in fairy tales but for some of us
folks we are not there and we go on day by
day looking for the time to say well at last I
think but I am not for sure but I do believe
that I have found the one I have been looking
for you know   The One*

By Donald Hoelscher

The Place

There are times when I think about that place of final peace with no more sorrow and no more pain to be with God in heaven again I do believe that in this world were put down here to meet a test that has been set down for all of us and that is why when the test is done he calls us to be with him in our own heavenly home

By Donald Hoelscher

The Place

There are times when I think about that place of final peace with no more sorrow and no more pain to be with God in heaven again I do believe that in this world were put down here to meet a test that has been set down for all of us and that is why when the test is done he calls us to be with him in our own heavenly home

By Donald Hoelscher

The Quandary

*I get up early every day but this morning I
decided in bed to stay and reminisce of things
in the past and wonder why they didn't last
oh well it's just another day and in my bed
I decided to stay and continue with the
thoughts of the old times and all the things I
left behind I believe that sometime we need
some special time to wish for what we left
behind people and places in the past and hope
the times that are yet to come will be good for
us and every one*

By Donald Hoelscher

The Ride

*I bought a car the other day it sounded good
I would have to say but as I drove it had a
noise so I took it to a mechanic for his advise
he passed the car and said that it was ok but
the noise I still heard was not ok so to a good
friend I did go and we took a ride and it
wasn't slow when we got back I was a wreck
for he had scared me half to death but all
in all the mystery was solved and a broken
spring was the last and final result*

By Donald Hoelscher

The Running Night

*There was a time when my nights were mine
and I could sleep all night but something
happened I don't know what but I am up at
several times a night so with this problem you
can see my nights no longer belong to me I saw
and add just today about a fellow who to all
did say I have this problem too I am telling
you I am on my way at least several times a
day they have a fancy word you know for all
this bladder flow but words don't change a
thing you know and the word is still go go go*

By Donald Hoelscher

The Sad Good Bye

Did you ever feel like you have lost a piece of you when someone says good bye and you feel like your worlds gone in a blasé as the time goes rolling bye and then the lonely ness just seems to press you down like a weight is on your mind and no matter how hard you try you know you just can't win so you pick up your broken heart and try to start again and remember what has gone before and what will be again so in memories you live and say once more again that I'll survive just one more time but where do I begin

By Donald Hoelscher

The Sad Theme

*Along time ago there was a child who came
to earth to save us all but people the way they
are would not believe that this was the long
awaited one so as a result they plotted to get
rid of him and so today when we have some
one that has a different outlook on life we plot
to silence them like of old and so the stories of
old are not so old for even today we have the
same scenario and people still plot to change
what is good for something mediocre*

By Donald Hoelscher

The Sad Truth

You get up in the morning glad that there here
and isn't very long for the sadness to appear
for words soon come out and you know it's
unreal and once more your back to what you
still fear to be alone is not what you need
but to be with someone you care about is so
nice indeed so once more you pack up your
pride and smile and once again try to hide
the thoughts that enter your mind and you
know that once more it will soon end and the
fear of alone will again soon began

By Donald Hoelscher

The Sale

I took a trip to town just to look around and
stopped at a place where several sales were
found and as I looked around I got a glimpse
at how the people lived and found a lot of
stuff that they had accumulated all a round
there was books toys clothes and knick knacks
and paraphernalia did abound but as I left
the place you can already see that some of the
stuff they had did go home with me

By Donald Hoelscher

The Short Day

Have you ever had a day when everything went wrong and no matter what you did it's the same old sad song and no matter how hard you try it seem that the time just seems to fly and what you intended to do just didn't seem to fly so if you have an answer I'd really like to know

By Donald Hoelscher

The Silver Spoon

*Did you ever once wonder what you would
be if everything you wanted would come to be
and your life would be totally stress free with
no cares or worries to be some time I wonder
as I look around just what it would be like to
be a clown and just be goofy and make silly
sounds or do weird things with people around
but such is the thoughts of a silly old man and
so as I end this pile of goofy thoughts ill keep
on wishing for my ship to come in or my rich
uncle to die in the poor house the end*

By Donald Hoelscher

The Single Life

I get up early with the sun shine and look out
my window just in time to see if by chance its
rain or snow or maybe the sun has decided to
shine and I tell myself it's not up to me and
like the rest will just have to see but until that
time I'll get myself dressed and hope not for
some company until I get dressed but there
are chores to do and I know that is true so I
best get to work and get the chores through

By Donald Hoelscher

The Smile

*In this world of pain and gloom there is
always room for some cheer just a smile can
always help even for the biggest grump and
there is always on the news things that will
seem to confuse and make us think the worlds
not right and that all we do is fuss and fight
but to me that's not what were about and
when you look into the face of a child it makes
you think for a wile of what the past we used
to be and could if all these cares and troubles
were set free I am sure that then we could be
like the child and have those smiles and once
more set them free*

By Donald Hoelscher

The Snow

I can still remember way back when if the snow did come the fun began and school was out and don't you know we all had our favorite places to go but that was then and life does change and the snow today has become a pain but sometime I wish I was young again and could do the things I did back then but this is now and not back then so we will just have to do our best and forget the foolish time we had back then

By Donald Hoelscher

The Spider

*This morning as I tried to dress I found a
spider in my shoe and as I wondered what to
do it startled me I am telling you the spider
then jumped off my shoe and started crawling
up my arm so as I looked down with some
alarm I put him where that he belongs I am
sure it will not happen with him again for
now he's met his very end so the morel of this
poem has to be check your clothes before you
get dressed to roam*

By Donald Hoelscher

The Storm

As I turned the TV on the weather man talked about a big old storm and warned it could possibly be bad and to buy some things you thought you had well a bottle of water a radio some kind snack food is always nice and to stay in side is always good advice but some folks like to watch the storm and the lighting as it dances round and watch the rain is it patters down and makes big puddles on the ground

By Donald Hoelscher

The Stumbling Stone

There are sometimes in our life when we have trouble in our life and the time for decision is close at hand but yet we still are not sure where we stand are if we stay or go to those of us who feel that way there is only one thing I can say is try to muddle on through the time and leave the past so far behind and live for a better day and remember never again to go that way

By Donald Hoelscher

The Thunder Rolled

*Last night as I laid in dream less sleep I heard
the storm into the area creep and rattle the
windows and the rain did sweep all the gravel
from my drive way take oh well I guess we
shouldn't complain for goodness knows we
do need the rain so once again the grass will
grow and we can again begin to start to mow
so buy more gas and don't be slow let's get
started now it's time to go*

By Donald Hoelscher

The Trip

*We packed the camper double quick to get
ourselves ready for the trip and soon we were
ready for to go and it seemed like the trip was
awfully slow and when we finally got to the
place we had to find our camping space to set
the camper up and soon we headed for the
pool to swim around for awhile and as the
day turned into night we went to bed   to try
it out and in the night it began to rain and
lightning and thunder rolled around and
there wasn't a dry place to be found the next
day we went on down to a concert farther
down the fireworks were a blast but after
that more rain came down we went on in and
laid on down and tried to sleep and listened
to the rains drip drip on the roof*

By Donald Hoelscher

The Unexpected

It's funny some time how what we wish for just don't seem to happen and what is not is what seems to take place I really don't know but it seems to me that we don't get what we wish for just look around and see I often wondered as I look around just what's next I wish that I knew

By Donald Hoelscher

The Why

Some time in this world we do some things
that defy explanation and the more we try
to figure it out the more baffled we become so
the best we can do is just stumble along and
try to live our lives and change the things we
can so I guess to end this story I'll say live life
one day at a time and fight one problem at
a time

By Donald Hoelscher

The Wish

*I wish once more that I could find a love
again like the one that's on my mind one to
last like the stories go that last forever as this
life goose some time in my mind I find that
love that's oh so true and fine but my dreams
are not real and to wake up a lone is no great
thrill I guess what I am trying to say that life
is not meant to live that way*

By Donald Hoelscher

There Is

There is a story in the bible I read about a
poor old lady that gave the best she had and
as I think about the story again I think of a
little girl that put in the only thing that she
had and somebody I really don't know who
took what she had given and threw it away it
was just play money but the only thing that
she had that came from her heart and that
can't be bad

By Donald Hoelscher

There is a dream

There is a dream we have in the back of our mind of things we would do if we had the time but most of us never really see it through and so its lost in this world we go through I often wonder if life isn't cruel In the life we go through its said there is an answer but I really don't know but sometime in the future ill hope to find if it's so

By Donald Hoelscher

There's a Place in Our Hearts

Well it won't be long Easter will be here and kids will be searching for things here and there mom and dad have lots of things to do to make sure the day is happy for all of you than its time for us to get ready for church and remember the Lord rose from the grave to save all of us and show that one day to he will bring us all back to be with him in the heavens above so let's not forget and remember the main reason for Easter this year

By Donald Hoelscher

There Was a Time

*There was a time a while ago when there was
not a reason to ask for any help so but that
time has passed and you need to ask for things
you need and hope for the best and you wait
and wait for them to arrive and maybe with
some luck you can survive and not go crazy
waiting there I guess this is the price that we
pay when we get older each and every day*

By Donald Hoelscher

Things to Do

Each day as you roll out of bed a myriad of thoughts run through your head and as you sit and ponder these things there is no hope of sleep again so you stumble around and try to wake up and head for the coffee pot then with some luck your finally a wake and you start thinking of your day

By Donald Hoelscher

Think

*As I lay there in my bed a myriad of thoughts
ran through my head of things I would like
to do and places I'd like to go but then the
reality of my life sets in and here I am once
again with thoughts of a better life with a
good and loving wife I wonder if this is again
to be or if this lonely life is all that will be I
am sure there is a better way to live this live
in a better place I guess the way to end this
poem is again to say I am still alone*

By Donald Hoelscher

This Crazy Life

You get up each morning and turn on the news someone has died and someone is abused I wish there was a day when someone would say there is no bad news or no more blues coming our way but that's not life I am sorry to say so put on a smile and a happy face to cover up your troubles and blues that's coming your way

By Donald Hoelscher

This Crazy World

*Every day you watch the news just to hear
something new but disappointment is all
you get and if its good It hasn't happened yet
so you change the station and sit and stew
about the bad things that have happened to
you and about the dreams you thought you
had at least it would help if they were not all
bad so I guess to end this gloomy day just take
a nap and forget the news and day*

By Donald Hoelscher

This Funny Life

*I once had a friend ship I thought would
never end but I have since learned that this
was not the case and the green eyed monster
had come to take my place well so much for
the friendship and if this is to be the way I
will be there no longer to even darken the
lady's door I will just have to find a friendship
somewhere else around where the green eyed
monster can no longer be found*

By Donald Hoelscher

This Goofy Life

*Once upon a time I had a dream of what my
life should be and then as fate would have it
all of the dream just went away some time I
think the fate is a cruel trickster that builds
us up just to take away it seems that the more
you plan the more it seems to be almost gone
or surely on its way it's been said that some
day we will know the answer but this is hard
to say*

By Donald Hoelscher

This Life

*Sometime I wonder in my mind what in
this life I am going to find each day seems
something new and life keeps on changing
too one day you're up the next your down
and than your stumbling all around it seems
like the older that you get the more you tend
to forget and things you know you should do
don't seem so important now and you put
them off again somehow so I guess what I am
trying to say don't let life get in the way*

By Donald Hoelscher

This Life of Ours

*This life of ours is filled with bumps and
humps and filled with lots of problems too
things like bills and such to torment and
trouble you and then we have the all alone
and what to do when your alone when you
are used to be with someone to share with
you your waking time and not be so all alone
things like a shopping spree or rummage sales
don't you agree are just a drive in the country
to see if when you saw it just yesterday if it's
the same or changed some way to be alone is
not so hot for then you realize what you're not
we can kid ourselves and say were just fine
and simply go gradually out of our mind and
live in a never never land but the solution is
to find a friend to be with you until the end*

By Donald Hoelscher

This Time

*Why are we here that's a mighty profound
question the answer to that depends on the
person who ask the question one might say I
do what I can the other will say I really don't
know I feel like we're all put here for to help
one another and the good book tells us who
is our brother and it isn't just the one who
is our mothers son but everyone we come in
contact with in need of help if we help with
a promise of reward than were paid but if
we accept no payment the reward is stored
in heaven by our god who sees all so where is
your payment*

By Donald Hoelscher

This World Today

I got a call just today about a love that went away its hard to believe that a love that was so strong turns out to be something that is now all wrong and people try to hurt one another just because of some simple blunder I don't understand how love can go away and turn to hate and melt away like snow on a bright sunny winter day

By Donald Hoelscher

Those Who

*There are those who think that I am fat but
I am not down with all of that but though I
would soon have to admit there's a whole lot
of me I would be the first to admit and some
time when I move around I find that things I
do does so confound and why the cloths that I
once wore no longer fit and it makes me sore
for surely I did something wrong for the cloths
I like feels like I am bound I'll bet a corset is
not so tight as the cloths I have on tonight*

By Donald Hoelscher

Time

*There is a time for all things and when the
time does arrive I know that I won't be alive
so if you would just leave me rest beneath the
shadow of heavens crest where I will lie until
the time the good lord calls me to come to my
final home up there on heavens shore*

By Donald Hoelscher

Time and Space

As we stumble in our race to be good and meet
the test we find that things get in our way and
slow us down or make us wait for things we
sure would like to have whether they be for
us good or bad all we know is that it's what
we want and don't care to be in the front of
some old messed up life were all there can be
is pain and strife so in our quest to be the best
we some time forget the ones we left behind as
they to stumble on along behind and trying
follow in our shoes

By Donald Hoelscher

Time of Year

Once again the time has come for parents everywhere to run to place things under the tree toys and gifts for you and me but some time I do believe that the message of Christmas is lost again you see for the message of Christmas is not the toys or the gifts beneath the Christmas tree but the message that god had sent his son down here for you and me I wish that we all could see what this means to you and me

By Donald Hoelscher

Tired

*Were you ever so tired that you couldn't hold
your head and even a whisper seemed like a
roar instead I can tell that this is true for I
have lived it through so if the chance should
come to you run as fast as you can for you will
pay big time at the very end*

By Donald Hoelscher

Tis Morning Again

*Time to get up my friend the day is dawning
and we are all yawing and rubbing tired eyes
and emitting lots of moaning and sighs why
can't the week end be longer with the week
being two days instead of five and we could
enjoy more bed time and lots of less tired sighs
oh well if that were the case the pay would be
less so I must confess me I need more not less
of a pay check I must confess so I will leave
time as it is and get up and go and rub my
eyes and say by by to the nice warm bed were
I laid my head for several long hours and quit
all the moaning groaning and sighs*

By Donald Hoelscher

To Do or Not

*As we grow up we know the way but somehow
we go astray and the things we know that we
should do are not the things we led to do so we
go on some time the wrong old way and even
when our conscience say you fool you know
that this isn't right we still persist and don't
do what's right oh well I guess all that there
is to say is today the devil got his way*

By Donald Hoelscher

Tomorrow

In this life of plans and schemas threes things that come to us in dreams of things that were and now are gone like the snow and rain after a big old storm and people too that once were here and like the snow they diaper but the memory of their lives remain to live again in our dreams

By Donald Hoelscher

Too Many Minds

*As I sit here in a daze I think about my younger
days and all the things that I once done and
all the ones and all the fun in dreams we live
in fantasies of times of old and things untold
of people and places in our past and wonder
why they didn't last I guess to live there in the
past when were old that's all we have so as I
close and say fare well I am not young and
you can you tell*

By Donald Hoelscher

Tracy

Some time in this crazy life we find a good friend that we like and so we hang on to this new found friend and help them in any way we can we are there when they are down and let them know that we can be found to help in any way we can

By Donald Hoelscher

Tragedy or Escape

*I woke up just a few mornings ago and saw all
the destruction the TV news did have to show
and wondered why this awful thing had to
happen but I guess that the things of the world
are not up to us for to know for nowhere in
the good book dose these happenings show
some time I wonder and I really don't know
if our God isn't calling all of them poor bodies
home*

By Donald Hoelscher

Trip to Space

I would like to board a big old rocket ship and travel to the heavens up above and search up there in the sky for my love that had to die but even if this was the case I would never find her out in space for there is but one place in the sky where we can't go unless we die so I guess I will stay here and do my best and hope to someday be blessed with a key to heaven's door where I can dwell forever more

By Donald Hoelscher

Trust

*Did you ever notice when a promise is made
how some folks seem to forget what they have
said and go on like nothing is wrong and leave
you hanging on the same old sad song like I
am sorry   I couldn't do anything to change
it we just got busy today and forgot the time
it just got away well sorry's ok once in a while
and even if you try to smile the feeling of hurt
just don't go away*

By Donald Hoelscher

Turn Back the Clock

Time keeps ticking day by day and if we're not careful it will slip away so live your life on and don't be shy for someday you will wonder why that you're not the person that you might of been if you would have just took the chance to live your life the way you want to start so when the chance is about to begin don't be shy just jump on in

By Donald Hoelscher

Vietnam Vet

*I am the boy who grew up next door and at
a very young age went off to war some of us
came home some did not some of us died and
still lay on the spot where we fell in a foreign
land to lay forever in our grave in the ocean
or on the land to serve our country was our
great plan so to those of us that did come
home I say treat us like that we still belong
don't turn your back on sons that come back
home but treat us like we still belong*

By Donald Hoelscher

Wake up

*As I woke up just today I heard the news
person have to say someone was killed on the
highway on the other side of town and schools
are closing near and far and as I listened on
to the news I can't help but wonder what this
world is coming to for I once heard that this
was the land of the free if this is true what's
happening to you and me for things that was
promised is not what's now and as far as I am
concerned the children are the ones that have
to pay for something that some fools do say*

By Donald Hoelscher

Wake Up Call

As we wake up our minds in a tighter and we scurry around trying to get our self's together with our kids still in bed and the clock keeps on ticking we know hurry's the thing but we can't seem to get things together I don't think it's the time maybe it's the weather or maybe it's the time we spent last night together I really don't know but I'll tell you what we just can't be late no matter what

By Donald Hoelscher

Walk Between the Drops

*I went to church just to day it was cloudy and
looked like rain as I sat in the church and the
mass began outside it had began to rumble
and looked like rain and then the drops soon
began so I slipped on out before the crowd let
go and headed home as fast as I could go for
I knew it wouldn't be to long before the sky
opened up and this old fat boy don't like to
run*

By Donald Hoelscher

Walk On

*I thought that I did have it made and then my
life went up in spades the life I had is now all
gone and here I sit all alone with no one here
but myself to blame and wondering how that
I can change and how I can go about to start
to fill my life with someone new and how to
tell that someone new is the one that I should
chose to get me out of this terrible place and
fill my life with a brand new start so once
more back in the breach and hope this time is
the last the one to take me home to live with
love and not alone*

By Donald Hoelscher

Way Back When

*I remember back in my Lost younger days a
family would come to visit and with us did
play we lived on a farm in a very small house
and the plumbing wasn't modern but just
and out house did suffice it had a long path
to the place in the woods with two holes that
beckoned and boy it was cold so if you had
business in that little house you better be
ready and get done quick and head for the
house lickety spit*

By Donald Hoelscher

We Find a Mate

*Like the birds and bees we search for a mate
and if you please were lucky and we do ok
but to some the world just seems the pits and
although we find what we think we really
want life comes along and changes it I wish
there was a magic pill that would help us
get up this big old hill and help us find the
one true love that's sent from the heavens up
above*

By Donald Hoelscher

Were Here Why

This is a question that I have and wonder yet today some people think they have the answer but me I am not too sure for everything you read seems to confound me more there is a passage in the good book that kind a points the way but even this is kind a vague and the only thought I have is the one that were all put here for a purpose and we spend all our lives doing this and that and we hope when it's our time we have finally found the purpose

By Donald Hoelscher

Wednesday

It was the middle of the week and hump day was here and the week end is closer and I am ready to cheer but there is still at least two more long days to endure before we can enjoy the bed a little longer to snore for five days a week its early to rise and rub all the sleep from very sleepy eyes and get out of bed and stumble around and watch the sad news of the rain coming down another sad week end of liquid sunshine well break out the umbrellas and a jacket this time

By Donald Hoelscher

Weeks

As the weeks go flying by it makes we wonder
if that I should do more of this and less of
that or more of that and less of this and spend
more time in the bliss of knowing life is not
a bother and try to be close to one another a
wise person did once say forget the past and
live for now, that's all we have there's no way
to change the past now all we have let's make
it last

Donald Hoelscher

Did You Ever

*Did you ever see it to fail when you're busy
doing something the door bell will buzz or
the telephone will start ringing off the wall
and its always some busy body wanting this
or wanting that and by the time you have sent
them on their way you're already out of the
productive mood you were in before all this
hubbub had begun well I guess the only thing
that can be said is it's just another day*

By Donald Hoelscher

Well It's Christmas Again

The time has come once again for people to call each other friends, and try again to start anew and do what our God wants us to do for he did come on Christmas night to set this world again back right and show us how to live again so we can be with him at the end So while we're here on this old earth lets always remember him and his birth and why he came to us down here to take away our sins and fear so we can have at least some faith, and hope again to be with him at our end.

By Donald Hoelscher.

Were Told

*When we grew up our parents told us we
should always do our best but they never
really told us that it would be such a ditch
and people that we had near us would stab
us in the back or they will even do us wrong
and act like they care and leave us all alone
and make some lame excuses of why they do
what they do oh well so they don't know the
golden rule they believe in take what you can
and forget about the rest*

By Donald Hoelscher

What Christmas Means

Is it the things beneath the tree are the smiles
of every one that you see are the smiles on the
children's faces or maybe and attitude of the
different places I wish that there was a way
to have Christmas here every day so everyone
would be happy and treat each other like the
good book says with love and respect in every
way my Christmas wish

By Donald Hoelscher

What If

*Just suppose we could have everything we
want and not just what we need and no longer
have a good reason to fret or greave and live a
life of happiness and bliss with all the things
we could ever want or possibly need I just
don't know if this would be good for wanting
things is a reason to live and to tell you the
truth I just don't think without these wants
and needs our life would be bad*

By Donald Hoelscher

What we believe

Why can't we get along and share each other's pain why are we so determined to be alone and suffer once again. We hide ourselves in our fears of a once very happy life. that we someday hope to share again with a husband or a wife and. why is that we smile and say there is nothing wrong and that our life is quite ok and we have known along when in our heart we know that some things just ain't right and that we have known the truth and have known so all along. Then we hide ourselves in the things we do each and every day and steal our self's for the night. for we know that in our dreams well have each other once again as lovers and best of friends

By Donald Hoelscher

What's in a Dream

A dream is good or a dream is bad its either very good or really bad it tells us of things that might have been or something that is yet to come have you ever been in a place you know you haven't been yet you know where everything is at or see someone you know that you haven't ever met and relive the conversation and know what is to be said before the words or out

By Donald Hoelscher

What's New

*Sometime in our lives we wake in a haze and
try to find an answer to these troubled days
and usually we find and answer but that's
not what it takes and the fog that's in our
mind only gets more troubling in our simple
days so to say that we are not confused would
be so out of place that we might as well go
on and stumble on our way for as a kid we
knew we had the answer but in our older
days were only more confused as we stumble
on our way*

By Donald Hoelscher

When

When you feel so down and your all alone
just think of the places that you've gone and
let those memories come back to you and live
the past that once was true for when your
down and feel alone there someone there that
was the one and they will see you through the
days and time especially when you're alone
and help you find that long lost love that
constantly dwells in your mind both night
and day and keeps you beat down that's all
I'll say

By Donald Hoelscher

When We Are Born

When we are born our journey begins and lasts through, our life with family and friends and ends when the Lord calls us away to be with him on some sunny day. all that can be said for that time and day is the time we are waiting seems such a long stay, and time we don't want to hurry along, for some day too our stay will be through and we will be joined by that heavenly crew and so we'll say good bye from Family and Friends

By Donald Hoelscher

When Were Young

When were young we think the world owes
us a living and everyone else does all the
giving and we have all the time in the world
to do whatever we want but as the time goes
quickly by one day we wake up and sigh hay
where's the time we thought we had and why
do I feel so bad and why are my friends going
away and leaving me with forlorn thoughts
of yesterday when my life was young and oh
so gay

By Donald Hoelscher

When you're Alone

*When your alone you have all these thoughts
and try to figure what life's all about but try
as we might there is no way we can even figure
out just this one day so all I can say is to do
your very best and let the good Lord take care
of the rest so as I end this simple refrain ill
ask you all to do the same*

By Donald Hoelscher

When you Awake

*When you're sleeping oh so tight and the phone
does ring sometime in the night especially
in the midst of a good old dream and you
enjoying it are so it seems you tend to be just
a little perturbed just to put it mild and you
try real hard to relax and smile but a smile
can't be seen at least on the phone and you
don't dare to let out a darn old groan so you
put on your best smile and talk so sweet and
try real hard not to bleat*

By Donald Hoelscher

Where

*There is a place where we can hide all of our
feelings deep inside and everyone knows the
place and it is not somewhere out in space and
it can't be found in our homes or anywhere
that we have roamed I bet if you think you
will find it to because it is somewhere inside
of you the place I mean is your heart where
all the joy, love, and pain does start*

By Donald Hoelscher

Where to Begin

I use to live for family now I am all alone the
people I called family are now out on their
own so now I sit a wishing I had to do what
my heart told me all along so what am I to
do to solve this lifelong song should I go out
to somewhere else and try to start again to re
establish me anew with some real close friend,
so I guess I'll try again for to start anew and
start to live for me or just for me and you

By Donald Hoelscher

Where to Go

*Where do you go when your worlds torn apart
and the part of your body that has keeps you
alive is broken to pieces by so many lies like ill
love you forever till death do us part then one
day as you wake up with a start you realize
finally that your once more alone and the
love you once shared has suddenly gone and
as your eyes fill with tears and you try not to
cry you still wonder and ponder the why
By Donald Hoelscher*

Where to Start

I don't know where to start when it comes to
this old lonely heart is it in my long lost past
or in our future right now someone please
tell me true for I don't know I am telling you
sometime there is a light that comes to me
in the night and lights my mind for a little
while and causes me to start to smile and feel
at peace for a little while

By Donald Hoelscher

While I Sleep

*The other night when I went to bed a visitor
came by and touched my head and told it was
time to be with my God and leave my family
and friends I ask if I might say good bye to
family and friends and he told me I had to
leave so I'd better begin so as they all gathered
I told them good bye and did so with tears in
my eyes for I knew that this was the last and
id have go and all they would have was our
happy past*

By Donald Hoelscher

Who Me

This morning as I woke up I heard this silly report good morning from a couple of Holstein cows and we all know that cows don't talk so what in the world is this all about all I can say is in all of my years and to this day cows haven't said a word so I really have to say some one sure has a silly imagination but it sticks in your mind its silly that way

By Donald Hoelscher

Who's Driving the Bus

I did once believe that the one in charge did drive you see but now I found that this is not so for the kids do drive I want you to know and it's a sad thing for the one in charge for he will soon be long gone because he stood up to the kids for you are not allowed to buck the bull at all and if you do your in for a fall for even the folks who are your support wont back up you are me so just ride in the bus and don't you dare to say a thing for it will come to bite you in the end so if you thoughts of driving a bus remember it's not you who is in charge

By Donald Hoelscher

Why Are

You see people rushing round pushing them self's right in to the ground don't they know that what we have is just borrowed and it's just down here I wonder as I look around at all the things that I see if some time that person could also be me The birds up in the trees they seem to have all they need and though they scurry left and right they have what they need each night

By Donald Hoelscher

Why God

*Some time I think God is real some time I just
don't know I really want to believe but look
what's happing around us so I know there is
a higher power and I know that's rightly so
but still I wonder why all these bad things are
happen to us down here below I guess I will
have to bide my time and try hard to believe
that all these things have a reason we must
all except what happens to us down below is
just part of the test to see if we are worthy of
a home up there above and where we can all
share the Lords forgiving love*

By Donald Hoelscher

Why Is This True

Take a look at this great plan and see the reason for the trouble that were in there's confusion everywhere and wars killing in the news and people wailing in there blues I wish I could change the way things are and get rid of pain and war but I know that there isn't any way so I guess that all that I can say is there sure must be a better way but it won't happen on this day

By Donald Hoelscher

Wishes

Some time when alone we wish that we were small and wouldn't have the worries and problems that that we have at all we could just sit around and play the whole day long and rely on someone else to help us get along but wishes are fleeting things and don't always come true so if I had a wish it would be for me and you

By Donald Hoelscher

Woman

*I would like to meet the man Who can say
they understand the women of this great land
and I would like to bet they haven't been
married yet and if they have and say they
can I would sure like to shake their hand for
I once thought I had a plan and found out I
had no clue to what a woman's going to do
for they live in a different world so if you
think you found a girl and she is the finest in
this world beware my friend for your in for
a mighty fall for you don't know them really
at all*

By Donald Hoelscher

Woman

*I would like to meet the man Who can say
they understand the women of this great land
and I would like to bet they haven't been
married yet and if they have and say they
can I would sure like to shake their hand for
I once thought I had a plan and found out I
had no clue to what a woman's going to do
for they live in a different world so if you
think you found a girl and she is the finest in
this world beware my friend for your in for
a mighty fall for you don't know them really
at all*

By Donald Hoelscher

Work Again

*We get up each day and sit and stew about
the problems we'll have before this day is
through and when we get home and were all
alone we think of how good it is ,to be once
more alone for this is the place we have been
all day and were we would stay if we had our
way but alas we must go to face another day
and again hurry home and once more to say
I'm Home!!*

By Donald Hoelscher

Working Slob

*I have heard it said that this country is in
need of lots of things and I do agree like help
for the working slob who goes to work every
day on a job and comes home Friday with
just enough to buy some food and pay his
rent he is the man who lives next door and
he will beg to feed his family that's for sure
he does his best to meet the test and thou he
tries some time he fails but Monday morning
he's on the job that's why some folks call him
the working slob*

By Donald Hoelscher

World Decorator

Did you ever look out as travel along and look at the wonders that our God has put on the grass and the trees all so green, and the beauty of the flowers in the early spring and my favorite is the snow in the winter with the world painted so white like the purity of morning In the dawns early light and the sky painted blue and the stars over head shining so bright down on me and you and that big old sun the warms up our days and that big old moon at night that guides our way this is the world our God gave to me and you so why so sad with all that our god has given to me and you

By Donald Hoelscher

Worry

Did you ever have a restless night when things were happing left and right and some were good some were bad but me I have been taught by the school of life that if there not bad they must be right so with this thought planted firmly in my mind ill jut go on to another day and time and leave the dreams in there behind its said the dreams are a prelude to what's right if this is true then I'll be alright

By Donald Hoelscher

Yet another Thanksgiving

It's once again Thanksgiving another year slipped away and together we gather and to each other say what on this day is there to be happy about is we're all a year older and hobble about so all I can say is at least I am still here at least for now in body even if the mind has disappeared

By Donald Hoelscher

Your Heart

*I do not mean the human heart but the one
that controls all our dreams and thoughts and
leads us on our fragile way to places where
we go astray we do things that we should not
do and leave alone what is right to do and
stumble on our haphazard way doing things
we should not do and leaves us both alone
and blue to find the person we should be will
take the whole eternity*

By Donald Hoelscher

Young to Old

*When were young we think each day that life
will always stay but then as time goes flying
by one day were a wondering why and what
happened to those golden years that people
talked about back in our younger years and
who is this old man that looks at me in the
mirror that I see it surely is not the man of
long ago that was always around when things
were slow*

By Donald Hoelscher

Younger Days

We send our kids on off to school to learn what we thought we knew but time just seems to take away what once we knew in our younger days there's things like memories gone bad and friends than we thought we had but like all things they go away and leave us blank in our older days so I guess the way to end this poem is to say hold on tight to them younger days

By Donald Hoelscher